DAVID

DAVID

KNOTS
MELTZER

TREE BOOKS

BOLINAS 1971

ACKNOWLEDGEMENTS: *"32 beams of light* was 1st issued as a Yes!Press free poem (ed. by Robert Durand) ; *"Tell them I'm struggling to sing with angels"* appeared in *Matrix:1* (ed. by aya;) *"Shaman denies fat pleasure"* appeared in an earlier version in *Measure:1* (ed. Howard McCord) ; excerpts from *Venice* were printed in *Tractor* (ed. Barbara Szerlip).

This book offered to my wife
& daughters & to my correspondent
in LA: JaH

Letters & Numbers

THIRTY-TWO (32) : Numbers of the Paths of Wisdom in Sefer Yetsira, consisting of the 10 Sephiroth & the 22 Letters of the Hebrew Alphabet.

*   *   *   *

In thirty-two mysterious paths of wisdom did the Lord create: He created His Universe by three forms of expression: Numbers, Letters, and Words.

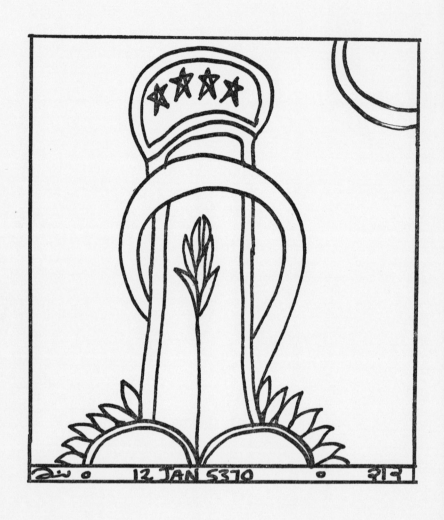

12 JAN 5370

1

In my 32nd year
counting numbers watching
22 letters dance on a wall chart.
Energy goes to & out of 10
ineffable sefira.
Electric radiant systems
I walk thru,
carry beneath my skin,
sing Paradise *Pardes*
walk down the path to help my wife
 (in green & gold light) carry
groceries back to our tree house
up 181 steps carved into earth

2

Twenty-two ways to speak,
tell you
God crowns spine's tree,
unwinds vertebral knots.
Light spreads thru flesh I
carry to our bed,
your loins spread
to accept the alphabet
I stutter into your womb

3

22 seeds take hold in your dark earth.
Shake apart into life.
22 seeds take hold, arise.
Life-fire rising up in bright loops
surrounds 6 points
unfolds into thousand petald celebration

4

Resting after love
beneath night's bridal ark
cobalt-blue lines outline your body
for the moment
600 thousand new sperm beings
float in the womb's sea

bright starlight
lights up the room

5

22 ways to pulverize the tongue
hack the serpent into 22
new snakes all with my face
the face of my children
busy with tongues that delight in song
argument questions
day & night
no stone unturned
no star unmarked
no life-line left in exile
all in all
22 ways

6

More than mere
utterance of 32 ways.
It must also be
22 seeds to germinate 22 new
Edens, Edom. Green
circles man returns to
as to the sea to re-
learn source.

7

Tracking down 32 lights
O eternal pinball metaphor
Electric-eyed whore
how we serve you
your round lights
service all your
magic numbers!

8

32 light beams break into rays on the page I
spread black ink over.
Designs, faces, secret code,
imagined Chinese, Hebrew,
Egypt glyphs, Nasorean,
Angel alphabets,
digests of all there is to know
reduced to letters to words.

All there is to know is all that I know.
When there is more
you shall have it.

9

This is the news brought back.
No mystery but in silence of numbers & letters.
I tell my bride
there is no mystery but the moment,
penetration,
when emanations merge & bind together.
Sun halves flaming,
stars inside-out,
the hills tremble
& the green glory of woods
turns desert.
No mystery but in the silence of
numbers & letters waiting our touch.
Infinite breath between each letter
sucked into the heart, each number,
each blacked-out star.

10

32 sequences
consequences
sing for you
to you
from toe to lotus.
Nerve-tree responsa.

[1969]

Pushing Through

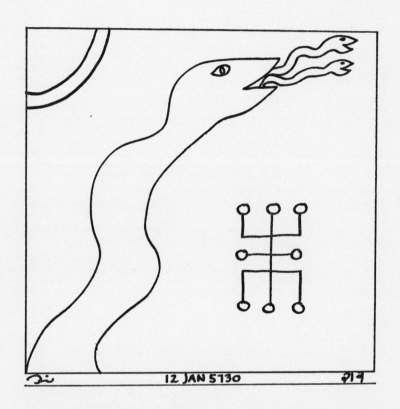

12 JAN 5730

PUSHING THRU

Pushing thru
       fast-dry cement
a fly
       dying to push thru
legs trembling
       death's web

           ●

Pushing thru
       underwater
5 minutes an hour no time
       heart beats
dynamite clock
       crystal alphabets
pearls worlds chains
       out of mouth & nose
eyes beaded w/ bubbles
       mirrors

       Pushing up against thru
grades of light
       sunray platforms
cut into water
       gravity against me
pushing thru

           ●

       Pushing thru
       stone wall
YAH mountainrange mirage
       surrounds the garden
ventric blossoms top root flame
       spread thru flesh O
                 pushing thru

           ●

       Pushing thru
base-knot fountain spine-route tantric
       progress linked to

coming into
        Eternity's diamond light
O penetration O
        pushing thru

[1969]

A. GOLEM

Adam Golem of heavy hands & feet.
Opens doors crashing thru them.
Grey rabbis look up in anger.
Shuts door slamming them.
Plaster walls crack with lightning.
Adam Golem, they sigh,
such a *klutz*.

●

Meets Lil under a gas streetlamp.
Instant horn for her.
Imagined *shofar* blows.
Lights her cigarette.
Mis-fires, turns her wig a-pyre.
Lil hollers, screams,
curses him into an accountant
doomed to sit upon a wire chair
counting atoms in Eternity.

●

Adam Golem finds mystery's key.
In atoms sees a grand thread
woven thru beads of universe.
Counts, sorts, adds it all up.

●

Flashbulb peeks at Paradise,
thigh-white flashes,
her mouth & eyes.
Shekinah reveals herself
from top to bottom;
Yod-built, her skin shines
light yielded by sun moon & stars.
Dark marks of her speech
come forth as gold & Adam Golem
walks across the honey bridge,
a swan, a tiger, a snake,
dissolves into a curled fist of being
unfolding slowly in her holy womb.
Adam Golem starts life anew.

[1969]

ONE

is what I am
always when I think about
what I am.

One.
Once & for all.
One.

One is also how I know
there are other ones too.
They always guide me
back & forth to one.
Once & for all.

TWO

is what I am
when I am
one with another one

like you & me in
the act of love.
Despite all the poems
we are one
we are two.

Two. Together
always one at a time.
Was it twice
we made love to each other
the other night?

Two is how we
understand one.

[1969]

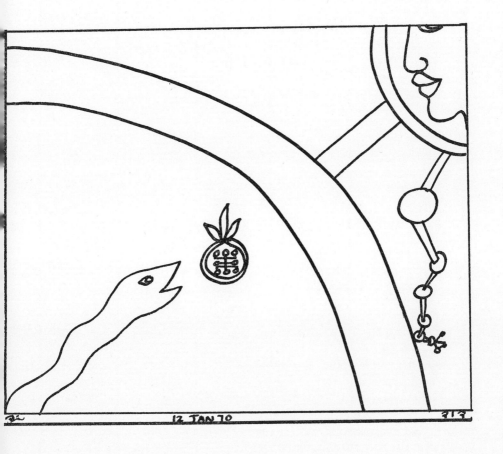

THE MATCHING, THE FUSION

The matching the fusion of earth within & without
of animal within & without
language within & without
specks & sparks
into the waterfall roaring out of my mouth

●

I want you within & without
my fingertips touch your nipples
I enter you within & without
our every fucking motion
within & without
breaks the seal
atom to atom
cell to cell
within & without
no limit
each body clear
each form space
fire aura compost
linked to ascension
perfection of white
perfection of black

●

Fern succulent petal
language
geology of face upon face
within & without
smear of infinity
snaketrack birdfeather
junco beak breaks thru my brain
lion of my name in my throat
tree trunk time ringed
sing the new song
within & without

Fern succulent petal
snaketrack birdfeather
O Queen of green sunlight
her gown a perfume of turned-over earth
babyskin in sunbeams caught

angel curve within & without
sparkle change
sweatdrop spermdrop dewdrop raindrop
sing the new song thru her vibrating center
visible invisible song
fern succulent snaketrack birdfeather
acorn berry babyskin

●

ALEPH, the first step
The end the beginning
inch deeper into her
within & without
plant exchange the instant letters
sunlight thru bedroom glass
dust cosmos riding back & forth
light lines layer our flesh
within & without
sun rods & shafts
cage our bed with alchemy
a prism made be entering you
you O you O Yod O Hay O sing the new song
sung thru Aleph sing
the matching the fusion
within & without

[1969]

Venice
13 Dec 69

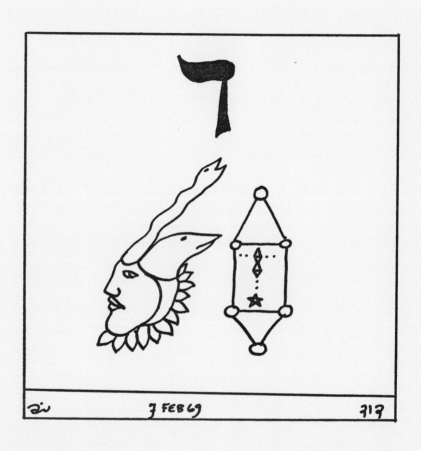

ש   7 FEB 69   דוד

A
1969

1

When we meet it's gangsters
passing crimes back & forth in public places.
Shaking hands, indeed!
Marathon baton runners,
we transfer looted crown jewels from palm to palm
then (quick!) into a leather bag
zipping thru your jacket sleeve
hooked to elastic thongs,
drops down a chute into boots
we clomp earth in, alone
by the sea or on neon boulevards
crowded with teenagers more naked than Adam.
All makers be apples shed by the Tree.

2

Light is the problem examined.
Natural vs fake light.
A link in Qumran scrools, cf
War of Light & Darkness, or,
before, in Ching glyph,
Ways To Test The Tao Dynamo.
We convene on Venice shores
where angels, gangsters, silver-screeners
zip & zap thru tired ruins,
tsimtsum across debris, parkinglots,
peer at us thru oilpump girders.
Shot-down, they shoot out venom curses,
buckshot amulets into the blue
blur of Lillith's wings.
Dazzle the sniper with a million flashlights.
An ever-ready light
emanates within the skin.
Lamp flame of inner oils
radiates in speech & touch.

4

Ghost clowns in a moviola dream.
Orchid creatures who grow & die in black & white
grainy rainfall of trapped atomic light
projected in The Movie on Fairfax.
In silents a light like the white
spaces around Raziel Abulafia's Hebrew letters.

Auras surrounding new root-shoots.
In silence
a light surrounds Buster Keaton's
monkey-light leap across Niagara,
falling to pluck love from sure death.
Silent light
poets & clowns bleed freely from the wound.

Gold-light burns
caught moonlight
in studio lamps
shining down
in photos
of Marilyn
        Monroe's last face.
        Each line holds Astarte's code,
        Eve's scars, Luna's pockmarks.
        Converges in coated-blue telephoto lens.

We are left at the end as it is in the beginning
only with images.

                    5
Lightbulb above my head.
LIGHTbulb inside my shell.
LightBULB glass dome unfolds
full electric bloom. The room
fills with shadow.
I'm en-lightened.
I see the Light.
EL light. AL light.
Light seeds sown in brain's dark.
Light blossom petals
radiant garden shines out of my eyes
this very moment.

                [1969]

B
1952–56

SUN LIGHT LA

17 years old
corpse pose
Savasan
on the bed, shades drawn
sun burns against window glass
curls papershades
106 Degrees
Heat Wave
blue-bottle fly

(1954)

SUN LIGHT NY

15 years old
flat on my back on the floor
ground floor flat
33rd & Third
bamboo curtains
absurd to read Plato
turn the radio on
Dodgers subdue me
steam phantoms curl up from Ebbets
dust bowl, top of the 7th
field a fast ball
turns into a pancake
wavering in space
Expands
fans scream
cheers turn to gravy
everyone a photograph
burning
no Bud, no Coke, no Her, no smokes
broke
outside the window, car horns
hack thru thick heat
samurai swords

[1952]

19
on a 3 day fast
dehydrated.

North wall dissolves into a gold hole,
flaming edges open out into a silver forest.
White-light treetops.
Platinum leaves shake off webs of mercury.
House-big snowflakes
wheel over moss-green mountaintops.
Sparkling rods grow in & out of buffed
aluminum planetoids, spheres
extend into infinity.

Inner angel says, "Go thru,
go thru the wall,
thru light's burning ring,
go to the other side,"
Over & over as night falls.

(1956)

C
1959

1

DiChirico without Cheracol
saw space where its dead echo opened-up
a plain unbroken by the dancers.
Instead
a relic supermarket nobody shops at.
Plaster-of-Paris bust of Augustus
Claude Rains Caesar face-down beneath
a Keinholz table
whose top is blue with Shirley Temples saucers,
pitchers. Mickey Mouse
wind-up dolls in rows like Detroit.
All tilt out of the running without electricity.
Veils of history,
garments worn in movies, hung on
steel racks at Costume R.K.O.
R. Karo would've used the tower's light.
He'd wear it as a cap to re-route lost energy.

A Yogi sits in space
above a white line dividing right from left
across a boulevard
named for a fly.
La Cienega.
Designed by DiChirico.
High-noon sun shines on the Yogi
3 inches off the road watching Eckhardt's DNA
bubble & re-fuse in the lights of the Milky Way.

The Pacific
starts & ends in electricity.
Neon feeds the Fun House signs,
klieglights shine on night-games,
juice for TV, radio.
Power milleniums come & go & die in the can
as Happy Ending rainbows fan auras over styrofoam palm trees
surround Studio City.

2

L'Age D'Or in a sportscar.
Wirewheels zoom thru funeral hills.
Radials screech thru Venice oil-fields.
Iron dinosaur skeletons bite into bruised clouds.

Speed thru it.
98 mph.
Mission-Orange late noon race thru the Hollywood Hills.
110 mph.
Swerve a curve onto the Freeway.
Into it, out of it,
we sit in a fireman-red Porsche Speedster.
Top's down.
Cut thru nomad towns.
Orchards, backyards, fields.
The driver is a moviestar.
We talk of Brahms & Mahler & Webern & Berg
& shit
of farmland ferment
stinks thru electric wire fences.
113 mph.
Pass by code-puffing diesel trucks.
Signs pass by,
lead you to Reno, Tahoe, Vegas.
Pedometer, speedometer, click new numbers every second.
120 mph.
Pass a ranch-style saloon
planted in a grove of gas-pumps.
124 mph.
Pass into dusk into night.
Smells like a whorehouse.
Night-blooming jasmine crushed.
Crash thru it.
Pass thru everything.
Hit a bump in the road
which is a rabbit.

3

The poet (me) sits on a bus-stop bench whose plywood back an-
nounces glory Forest Lawn where Angelo's David looks over the dead
piled in stacks feeding bone-rich soil greened with creamy astro-turf.
I sit eating green & dusty seedless grapes, Thompson's, 2 lbs for 25c,
bought at Ralph's on Western whose insides shine with meat redder than
Christ's blood rivers of guilt. Cans, boxes, bags, radiating hypno-art,
hyᵣe-rape smiling on chrome-trim shelves. Music surrounds you, unties
the mind, a soundtrack, we are all in air-conditioned beauty, moviestars
at last, buy buy buy. My eyes dive into mirrors multiplying visions of
perfect fruits, vegetables, shine in refrigerated displays trays untouched
by mite or fly or ladbug or earwig. A man in surgeon-white walks up &

down aisles spraying the food-wheel every hour on the hour. 24 times
day. We never close. Nothing dies.

4

HOLLYWOOD ROXY HOTEL SNAPS

It's an Oklahoma moon,
full & golden,
a bubble of wheat seed
hangs over Hollywood & Vine
like a zeppilin.

        *   *   *

Reaching up to spear the full moon,
    red-nosed antenna,
K.L.A.C.

        *   *   *

Plays his Stella 12 string in memory of hills
joined by car horns along Hollywood Blvd.
He sings *Your Cheatin' Heart* in the hotelroom
No Noise After 10 & his E-string is out of tune.

        *   *   *

Kissing the producer's hard shoulder bone,
her lips rub against the glass of mirrors.

        *   *   *

Old man's new moon
cataracts he sees thru on the dark
    porch of the Hollywood-Roxy Hotel.
Chews a dead Muriel, drop of yellow on his bib.
    Stars, ghosts, sperm-white shadows
move back & forth across the dim lens.

[1959]

Tohu

Tohu is a place which has no color and no form, and the esoteric principle of "form" does not apply to it. It seems for a moment to have form, but when looked at again it has no form.

ZOHAR, 1/16a

ADMONITIONS

Stay away from these words & all other words
in dark books or books too easy to find.

●

You dont need a teacher.
You're without a lover.
You are a bride in a painting.
No one penetrates you.
Your hymen, in time, will turn to brass.

●

Take the Greyhound out of town.
Take up tree-reading.
Telephone poles.
Wires a calligraphy
untangled by clear thought.
Remember,
imagination breaks the code.

[1969]

THE FIRE

"A funeral will be held for them.
We will form a procession
And I will tear my coat
And we will bury them
Just as in a funeral for a human,"
says Rabbi Zadle Leshinsky after the fire.
The books burnt:
3 sacred scrolls,
a 600 year old Mishnah,
a Torah annotated by Maimonides,
an early Kabbalist text
"damaged beyond use."
Well-used books on shelfs in shul,
in the Rabbi's study,
piled on each other like lovers,
the pages thumbed to a time-worn tissue
light is filtered thru.

Fire lights nothing.
It is the light below the light longed for.

Fire turns the page to ash.
Ash in turn is turned into soil
to feed the Tree.

All burns down around the fool.
No Jeremiah, no prophet, no one comes
to suck in smoke & fire,
spit out flame webs
shaped into Heavenly rooms
we could spend Eternity
walking in ever-changing splendour.
Door after door to be opened.

Everything burns down.
Fire serpents bark from exploding bowels of
raging demon dogs.
Fire crashes thru walls like fists.
Bores thru books like light beams.
Words radiate, then expire.
Windows melt back to sand.
I sit room-center piloting the angel-ship
bend towards Paradise.
I read:
"The soul unites with the divine soul in a Kiss."
Ceiling folds up, falls on the chair,
cracks open my skull like a walnut.
Vision over, done with.
12 angels band together
& hose the fire off my skull.
Vision speeds from the room with smoke
pulled back into space,
back into worlds behind worlds
within the rings I work my art thru.

[1969]

I'm forever lost in beginnings.
Each day I clear the table,
sweep books off the shelf,
throw pages into the fireplace.
At night hunt thru ashes
for an unburnt page to read,
one word to start it all over again.

*　　*　　*

The obstacles are in the mind inventing them.

*   *   *

It all boils down to a basic process of boiling it all down.
Keep vitamins in tact.
Swallow every drop. Each sup is NOT the same; it is NEVER the same.
Keep tasting until the tongue discovers itself
wed with an elegant serpent twined around Etz Hayyim whose roots weave thru earth, a tight-knit cap upon Kadmon the Poet's Adamic skull;
his words when used right have fish-hooks in each vowel that snare eye's membrane; his words on parchment are thousands upon thousands of sharp teeth shredding psyche into dust sprinkled over Eve's snowwhite thighs;
emanations light the body up & contractions re-track it back to root pumping oceans fuels into soup-stock boiled-dwn in iron kettle
placed before you in a brown earthen bowl whose glazed sides are graved with cranky Aramaic dream manifestos that embrace & guard the vitamins.
It is NEVER the same.
Keep tasting.

*   *   *

Power-failure.
Bartok silenced in *Mikrokosmos,* Book Two:
Minor 6ths in Parallel Motion.

The left side of silence lit by a kerosene lamp. The right lit by a fat white scented (clove) candle on of the kids brought from a mail-order Voodoo Shop advertised in *Fate.*
The 2 flames cross-hatch.

*   *   *

Outside: wind & rain.
70 mph wind off Mt Tam knocks telephone poles down like stonge-henge dominoes.
Right in the middle of writing a poem.
Power-failure.
After all these years at it, you'd think I'd know touch-typing.

*   *   *

Half the apple's in my mouth, the other half
still stuck to the branch,
bends with my body. I

dangle over familiar voids.
Words & angels gang together,
watch, whisper, take bets, pray.

* * *

Power is turned back on.
Shuttle thru the shell of old worlds into the new.
Bela touches down on the keys.
The phone rings.
Someone at the other end hears me say hello. But doesnt answe
back. Silence at the other end in the other place. Serpent mystery hisse:
Static. The other place.
All of the other places. In the imagination. Beyond the eyes & ear
Lost in millions of miles of circuits & wires.

* * *

[1969]

Tell them I'm struggling to sing with angels
who hint at it in black words printed on old paper gold-edged by time
Tell them I wrestle the mirror every morning
Tell them I sit here invisible in space
nose running, coffee cold & bitter
Tell them I tell them everything
& everything is never enough
Tell them I'm another cross-wired babbling being
songs coming out all ends to meet & flash above the disc above my brain
Tell them I'm a dreamer, new-born shaman
sitting cross-legged in trance-stupor
turning into the magic feather contemplated
Tell them there are moments when clay peels off my bones
& feeds a river passing faces downstream
Tell them I'm davening & voices rise up from within to startle children
Tell them I walk off into the woods to sing
Tell them I sing loudest next to waterfalls
Tell them the books get fewer, words go deeper
some take months to get thru
Tell them there are moments when it's all perfect
above & below, it's perfect
even moments in between where sparks in space
 (terrible, beautiful sparks in space)
are merely metaphors for the void between
one pore & another

[1969]

Shaman denies fat pleasure.
Holes-up in a cave to fast.
Ghost animals come at night &
sing ghost animal songs about
Animal Heaven where earth is meat
on a firey bone devoured
hour after hour in the barking Void.
Shaman deciphers each whine & yowl.
He deciphers light songs sung by
the farthest star, the nearest spark.
Reads a quick light flash
passing over loon's eyes.
Shaman de-codes all glyphs & gyres
& translates rainbow tract
dazzling in dragonfly's spread wingspan.
Shaman bent over each vowel like a watchmaker.
Flame-crazed by code, see him crawl
ever hallucinating boulders & bake in the sun.
See Shaman go for words where no words are.
Frozen lightning in rock,
crystal ideograms his fists pick at.
He digs into hot earth batter.

O let earth & all earth's critters know
I was here & I am her's too
Make use of me, sweet Mystery
Make use of me from toe to lotus!

       Days later
see Shaman in no-self daze
stumble into town
xylophone-ribbed, tobacco-leaf brown.
People make room for Shaman,
watching all his moves with inner cameras,
confused how his bloody fingers move out
to touch invisible shapes
he alone sees.
Shaman knows beyond knowing
Shaman knows man beyond man
& when Shaman is ecstatic & righteous
Shaman sings a song that is the song of earth.
There is no better one.

[1970]

Notes For Asaph

A Work in Progress

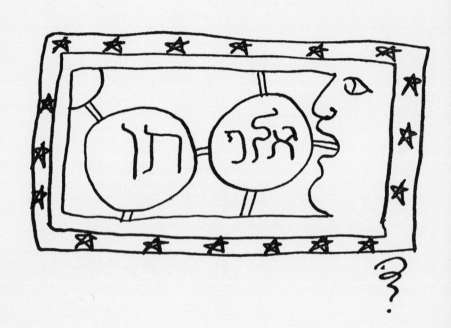

ASAPH (or Asaf or Asof) was David's chief musician.
A cymbal player.
      Play the cymbal
           David, the symbols, poet
         each breath a chance,
              a change born of pulse.
"There are no closed systems in nature"
     no sure thing
          in music, the poem,
the ground we stand on constantly shifts.
We intone notes. Black dots on paper
guide our throats open, let out song,
sound tones of transforming noise.
      "I am making you a spirit," sings the Chippewa
         on earth in harmony with chance
          the changes, chants.

       *   *   *   *

      Asaph fronts the Jerusalem Percussion Band,
his brass cymbals
     clash in desert air, light
flashing code to devout who transcribe it
     from tower to tower, the relay
a dance across the plains.
     "Praise HIM upon the well-tuned cymbals;"
praise HER upon the harp.

      Gliding down the Nile thru green harps,
bamboo brushing by like fiddles,
counterpoint of outstretched ibis wings,
black & white flashing in the grey spray.
David's basket snags in bracken, braked by weeds.
The Black Queen hears him, a nest of birds,
cooing for mamma, & with her ladies,
alert to such signals,
goes to music's source.
They clothe him as we close systems.
Play on cymbals, sign time,
mark lines with dots,
do service with devotion.

       *   *   *   *   *

We examine the structures, CONTAINERS,
        vestments, monuments, FORMS

the symbol nimbly fumbles it.
Always chase downhill.
                Old Man Ribber, trickster adventure,
                Shinn-bull. The struggle
                as cricket against cricket hind
                        is music made, is music any less than the ear
                letting it thru.
                        We need only open ears,
                                open our throats.
It passes thru like light as song.

                *   *   *   *   *

                The language of music is letters
                The music of poetry is letters

                *   *   *   *

Rhythm: strophe
Isotope: strophe
Tone : strophe
Cata
        strophe, growls Durante at the upright,
head wagging back & forth,
fingertips the nerve, we are instrument
made by musics tracked down on the page.
The letters.
Each black circle an inkwell holding harmony.

Rods of music molecules
        lines atoms ride on, Adam
light the speck pronounces,
        song the light condensed
in letters striding straight ahead on
        horizontal lines
                        "Perspective"
the painter calls the curve where
music the rider gallops away
into infinity.

                *   *   *   *

                It's a music your head hears
                        makes time move into place,
                "the sounds of a time." We are
                        a sound-tracked people

&, as royalty, music follows us
       wherever we go.

           *   *   *   *

       Singing together
our 2 voices (I see them
       on an oscillator) merge
into a rippling green light band,
       2 electric snakes entwined,
combined, converge.

Afterwards, song over, we say,
"That buzzed, that really rang."
A vibration tuned our voice to song,
a transfusion,
       a moment to moment transformation,
as air as light came
           sudden thru the dusty window. Sun shift.

           *   *   *   *

It was 1947
       Heaven abolished by atomics
a young David, Asaf's fable
       in conspiracy with my father
walked Broadway thru stores in quest of
       a proper bop beret to wear to
the Royal Roost to
       hear Bird blow.
The beret was soft felt,
       chartruese, & young David
(I wanted a burgandy cardigan too)
       felt crowned by the neon green
& took his place at the bar in the smoke
       to serve witness to the music.

           *   *   *   *

Yes it must've been grass, a joint they passed
       around the small Royal Roost stage
in darkness of God, klieg fragments of fallen
       angels who by Samael's design
find themselves at ringside, an audience to rites
       their heads can not.

           *   *   *   *

Django the Gypsy the lion Rousseau
          painted awake in green dream jungle
Cotton Club Afrique
          leopards & panthers
in harmony with golden snakes
          wrapped around magic trees

                    *   *   *   *

Play jazz all day & night
JAZZ the speech of atomas, Adamah
JASS electric exchange of greeting
meeting her head & toe in
CREATION, FORMATION,
IMPROVISATION
poet's art musician's art
all know what it is (means) to
follow it out to final form O
TREE OF LIFE

                    *   *   *   *

All my troubles double in morning
          rubble at night, stubble to shave
raining poem of pain & Rhythm Boys
          tape-loop, *A Bench in the Park,*
Rinker, Barris & Harry Lillis
          Crosby (Bing) sing
as pain rains light needles,
          poets need to give pain form.
                    Then sing!
                    day & night

                    *   *   *   *

Spring brings infinite noise
          Sparrows of 5 varieties perch on fushcia branchings
California bluebird brings nest grass to the backyard birdhouse
          2 Scrub-jays perch on garage shingles
                    an albino sparrow fluttering in the pines
all of them, their song, their eyes (says man on earth)
          watch me sun, read Jane Ellen Harrison
                    intermittently.
                    When I look up (as if looking were hearing)
to locate new bird choir soundings from trees beyond the fields
          (& Crows squawking on telephone wires)
                    sudden fart of band-saw starting-up &,

as usual, I think it's another damn fool on his Sear's dune-buggy
    or mini-bike setting-out on Elm to prove he's
        louder than God. But
it's a band-saw alright
        pruning a tribe of eucalyptus to the ground.
It goes on & on until all the birds stop singing.

                [1971]
                Bolinas

Five hundred copies published in Santa Barbara at
Christopher's Press & printed by g. e. albers
September 1971

CHEMISTRY OF THE EARTH

KARL K. TUREKIAN *Yale University*

HOLT, RINEHART AND WINSTON, INC.
New York   Chicago   San Francisco   Atlanta
Dallas   Montreal   Toronto   London   Sydney

Editor's Foreword

Physical science and technology in themselves bring neither salvation nor doom for mankind. Rather, they are as much a part of man's cultural environment as poetry and music. The comprehension of the physical world and its harnessing are no less acts of the human spirit than the creation or appreciation of works of art.

This series presents fundamental knowledge of our physical world in as elementary a way as the editors and each author thought possible, without reducing the presentation to banality. Not all parts of the books can be read with equal ease. However, just as there is no effortless way to learn to play the violin well, there is no way to comprehend nature without applying oneself to the task. It is hoped that through these books the reader will not only discover the beauty of the physical universe, but will also learn about the processes that lead to an understanding of the universe.

The series format permits teachers and students to choose the material to suit their own aims and interests.

KARL K. TUREKIAN
J. RIMAS VAIŠNYS
Editors

Orville of Yale University reviewed Chapters 4 and 5 and his criticisms are gratefully acknowledged. While thanking my critics, I must also absolve them of any blame for errors in the book that may have crept in despite their diligently given advice.

I thank my wife for following the development of the book and trying continuously to impose on my exposition the point of view of the nonscientist.

Mrs. Ann Phelps typed the manuscript.

K. K. T.
New Haven, Conn.
March, 1972

Preface

One can view the earth from many perspectives: its place in the universe, the history of its life, or the chemical and physical qualities it displays. In this book I focus on the various ways one can view the earth—its past, present, and future—from the chemical point of view. I have presumed that for the student with a minimum scientific background the development I have followed will present an understanding of the chemical nature of the earth.

Chapters 1 through 3 introduce the concept of matter, how it may have formed in the array we see it now and what laws govern its interactions. Chapters 4 and 5 discuss the solid state of matter observed in the earth as minerals and rocks. Chapter 6 presents an overview of the distribution of chemical species in the various parts of the earth. The time dimension for processes on the earth can be metered by using radioactivity, and this topic is dealt with in Chapter 7. The origin and history of the earth are then discussed in Chapter 8. The Epilogue, Chapter 9, presents a short statement of my views on the consequences of man's interaction with his earthly environment. Two appendices, one on phase diagrams and the other a listing of some useful constants and conversion factors, are included to be of assistance to the student.

In order to keep the book of reasonable size as a paperback, not all subjects were treated in as much detail as would have been desirable. In particular weathering processes and reactions in aqueous media are subjects that deserve far greater space than I was able to give them. No detailed examples of rock dating are included because of this self-imposed space restriction. It is hoped, however, that the principles are presented in a reasonably adequate way in most chapters to permit an introduction to the entire field. A short list of books and journal articles for further reading is given at the end of each chapter. As much as possible, current paperback books which might be particularly useful are included. Companion volumes to my book in this Physical Science and Technology Series are clearly R. B. Gordon's *Physics of the Earth* and A. G. W. Cameron's *Structure of the Universe*. Both of these books treat in detail certain aspects of the earth that are covered lightly in my book.

The manuscript in part or in whole was read critically by several people and I have benefited from the various suggestions made by them. I am particularly grateful to Professor Leon Long of the University of Texas for his detailed criticisms. Professor Phili

Contents

1 The Elements

Through the ages, man has tried to uncover the fundamental, irreducible units that together make up the material universe. From the time of the ancient Greek philosophers to the present era of high-energy accelerators, the quest has continued. The answers have ranged from the four "natural" units – air, fire, earth, and water – to the sophisticated array of particles reported by today's nuclear physicist.

Yet throughout time, man has interpreted the world about him in terms of his own practical needs. Hence, gold, silver, iron, tin, and the other "elements" – each a part of man's day-to-day experience – early became the practical expressions of his view of the substance of the universe. To most men today, an extension of this attitude identifies the totality of the *chemical elements* as representing that irreducible stuff.

Although the first systematic listing of the chemical elements and their properties – in the form of a "periodic chart" – was not made until the nineteenth century, a crude classification had been in use long before by ancient metallurgists who distinguished between "base" and "noble" metals as well as more refined but principally anthropocentric subdivisions. Inquiry into the nature of these "basic" building blocks, the chemical elements, culminated in the concept of the *atom*.

THE STRUCTURE OF THE ATOM

A picture of the nature of the atom is derived from a variety of physical observations. From these the model of the atom, as composed of a positively charged central *nucleus* about which negatively charged *electrons* move in an orbiting fashion, emerges. The simplest atom having one electron revolving around a central nucleus, is of the chemical element called hydrogen. The positive charge of the nucleus exactly balances the single electron's negative charge. The nucleus of the hydrogen atom has the smallest mass and the smallest positive charge of all atomic nuclei and is called a *proton* (Fig. 1-1).

In a neutral atom the *proton number* (the number of protons in the nucleus) is matched by an equal number of orbiting electrons. The proton number determines

1

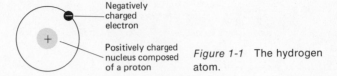

Figure 1-1   The hydrogen atom.

the chemical properties of an element. Hence, for example, all nuclei containing only one proton are identified chemically as the element hydrogen. By using a sensitive instrument called a mass spectrometer (Fig. 1-2), we can show that there are other atoms with the same chemical properties as the simple hydrogen, but having masses two or three times its mass. Since there is only one proton in the hydrogen atom, and since there must be only one electron balancing this charge, another type of particle must be present, in the nucleus, that increases its mass without altering the charge. In fact, this new particle does have a mass about equal to the proton's and is electrically neutral. It is called a *neutron*.

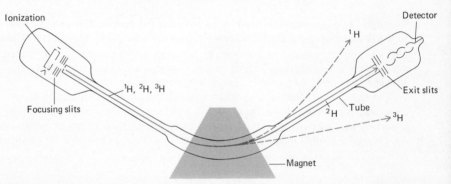

Figure 1-2   The mass spectrometer. The magnet field strength determines the mass focusing on the detector.

Neutrons have been generated outside the nuclei of atoms by means of a variety of devices. The most common one is the nuclear reactor, used now for power production as well as scientific research. The addition of a neutron to a proton, forming a hydrogen atom (called *deuterium*) with a nuclear mass about twice the mass of the simple hydrogen atom, has been performed in the laboratory. Adding still another neutron to deuterium results in a hydrogen with a nuclear mass of about three times the mass of the simple hydrogen atom, called *tritium* (Fig. 1-3).

^{1}H "Proteum" ^{2}H "Deuterium" ^{3}H "Tritium"

e = electron
n = neutron
p = proton

Figure 1-3   The isotopes of hydrogen.

We can now expand the discussion to include all the chemical elements and to arrive at some useful definitions. We think of the nucleus of an atom as composed of two types of primary particles: the neutron, with a charge of zero, and the proton, with a positive charge equal in size to that of an electron. These two nuclear constituents are called *nucleons* and have about the same masses.

Beginning with these building blocks, we can define any observable assemblage of nucleons in nuclear form as a *nuclide*. No matter how transient the assemblage of nucleons may be, it is considered a nuclide if it is observed by any of the instrumental techniques available to nuclear scientists. Nuclides having the same number (Z) of protons (or "proton number") but different numbers (N) of neutrons are called *isotopes;* those having the same number (N) of neutrons but different numbers (Z) of protons are called *isotones;* and those with the same number of nucleons (that is, the same "mass number") (A) are called *isobars.*

As an example let us consider the three adjacent chemical elements, argon ($Z = 18$), potassium ($Z = 19$), and calcium ($Z = 20$). The *isotopes* of argon with $N = 18$ and $N = 22$ have mass numbers (A) of 36 and 40, respectively. Argon with a mass number (A) of 40 is *isobaric* with potassium with a mass number (A) of 40 ($Z = 19$, $N = 21$), and calcium with a mass number (A) of 40 ($Z = 20$, $N = 20$). *Isotones* are argon with $N = 22$ ($Z = 18$, $A = 40$), potassium with $N = 22$ ($Z = 19$, $A = 41$), and calcium with $N = 22$ ($Z = 20$, $A = 42$).

Each element has a symbol, as is shown in Table 1-1 (for example, H = hydrogen, He = helium, K = potassium), and is characterized by a unique proton number. If the isotopic identification is important to a problem it is the common procedure to give the *mass number* as part of the symbol. Hence the three isotopes of hydrogen are written ^{1}H, ^{2}H, ^{3}H, indicating mass numbers of 1, 2, and 3, respectively.

NUCLIDES AND NUCLEAR REACTIONS

In dealing with atoms, we must become accustomed to thinking about dimensions considerably smaller than those in our everyday experience. To give an idea of these dimensions let us view the element gold on the atomic scale. Using the proper instruments, such as a mass spectrometer mentioned above, we can determine that gold atoms have about 197 times the mass of the simple hydrogen atom. That is, if we say that the *atomic weight* of hydrogen (dominated by the simplest isotope) is 1, the atomic weight of gold is 197. In order to convert this to an absolute mass unit instead of a relative unit, we modify the phrase "atomic weight" with the appropriate mass unit. Thus we could have the *pound atomic weight* in the English system or, in the metric system, the *gram atomic weight*. The gram atomic weight is the unit used exclusively in chemical and physical calculations. Since, by definition, 197 grams of gold has the same number of atoms as 1 gram of atomic hydrogen, that number of atoms is called the *mole*. The number of atoms in a mole is constant, independent of the gram atomic weight of the nuclide, and has been determined to be 6.023×10^{23} atoms per mole. This is called Avogadro's number.

If one mole or 6.023×10^{23} atoms of gold weighs 197 grams, each atom then must weigh

$$\frac{197 \text{ grams/mole}}{6.023 \times 10^{23} \text{ atoms/mole}}$$

or 3.3×10^{-22} gram.

Table 1-1   Distribution of Electrons in Neutral Atoms According to the Aufbau Principle (p. 11)

Element	Symbol	Proton Number	K	L		M			N				O			P			Q
			1s	2s	2p	3s	3p	3d	4s	4p	4d	4f	5s	5p	5d	6s	6p	6d	7s
Hydrogen	H	1	1																
Helium	He	2	2																
Lithium	Li	3	2	1															
Beryllium	Be	4	2	2															
Boron	B	5	2	2	1														
Carbon	C	6	2	2	2														
Nitrogen	N	7	2	2	3														
Oxygen	O	8	2	2	4														
Fluorine	F	9	2	2	5														
Neon	Ne	10	2	2	6														
Sodium	Na	11	2	2	6	1													
Magnesium	Mg	12				2													
Aluminum	Al	13				2	1												
Silicon	Si	14				2	2												
Phosphorus	P	15		10		2	3												
Sulfur	S	16		neon core		2	4												
Chlorine	Cl	17				2	5												
Argon	Ar	18				2	6												
Potassium	K	19	2	2	6	2	6		1										
Calcium	Ca	20							2										
Scandium	Sc	21						1	2										
Titanium	Ti	22						2	2										
Vanadium	V	23						3	2										
Chromium	Cr	24		18				5	1										
Manganese	Mn	25		argon core				5	2										
Iron	Fe	26						6	2										
Cobalt	Co	27						7	2										
Nickel	Ni	28						8	2										
Copper	Cu	29	2	2	6	2	6	10	1										
Zinc	Zn	30							2										
Gallium	Ga	31							1	1									
Germanium	Ge	32							2	2									
Arsenic	As	33		28					2	3									
Selenium	Se	34		copper core					2	4									
Bromine	Br	35							2	5									
Krypton	Kr	36							2	6									
Rubidium	Rb	37	2	2	6	2	6	10	2	6			1						
Strontium	Sr	38											2						
Yttrium	Y	39									1		2						
Zirconium	Zr	40									2		2						
Niobium	Nb	41									4		1						
Molybdenum	Mo	42		36							5		1						
Technetium	Tc	43		krypton core							6		1						
Ruthenium	Ru	44									7		1						
Rhodium	Rh	45									8		1						
Palladium	Pd	46									10								
Silver	Ag	47	2	2	6	2	6	10	2	6	10		1						
Cadmium	Cd	48											2						
Indium	In	49											2	1					
Tin	Sn	50											2	2					
Antimony	Sb	51		46									2	3					
Tellurium	Te	52		silver core									2	4					
Iodine	I	53											2	5					
Xenon	Xe	54											2	6					

Table 1-1—(continued)

Element	Symbol	Proton Number	K 1s	L 2s	L 2p	M 3s	M 3p	M 3d	N 4s	N 4p	N 4d	N 4f	O 5s	O 5p	O 5d	P 6s	P 6p	P 6d	Q 7s
Cesium	Cs	55	2	2	6	2	6	10	2	6	10		2	6		1			
Barium	Ba	56	54 xenon core													2			
Lanthanum	La	57														2			
Cerium	Ce	58	2	2	6	2	6	10	2	6	10	1	2	6	1	2			
Praesodymium	Pr	59										2			1	2			
Neodymium	Nd	60										3			1	2			
Promethium	Pm	61										4			1	2			
Samarium	Sm	62										5			1	2			
Europium	Eu	63										6			1	2			
Gadolinium	Gd	64			46							7			1	2			
Terbium	Tb	65			1s to 4d							8	8	5s, 5p	1	2			
Dysprosium	Dy	66										9			1	2			
Holmium	Ho	67										10			1	2			
Erbium	Er	68										11			1	2			
Thulium	Tm	69										12			1	2			
Ytterbium	Yb	70										13			1	2			
Lutetium	Lu	71										14			1	2			
Hafnium	Hf	72	2	2	6	2	6	10	2	6	10	14	2	6	2	2			
Tantalum	Ta	73													3	2			
Tungsten	W	74													4	2			
Rhenium	Re	75					68								5	2			
Osmium	Os	76					hafnium core								6	2			
Iridium	Ir	77													9				
Platinum	Pt	78													9	1			
Gold	Au	79	2	2	6	2	6	10	2	6	10	14	2	6	10	1			
Mercury	Hg	80														2			
Thallium	Tl	81														2	1		
Lead	Pb	82														2	2		
Bismuth	Bi	83					78									2	3		
Polonium	Po	84					gold core									2	4		
Astatine	At	85														2	5		
Radon	Rn	86														2	6		
Francium	Fr	87	2	2	6	2	6	10	2	6	10	14	2	6	10	2	6		1
Radium	Ra	88																	2
Actinium	Ac	89																1	2
Thorium	Th	90					86											2	2
Protactinium	Pa	91					radon core											3	2
Uranium	U	92																4	2

This small size is not practical when dealing with problems on the nuclear level; hence a more manageable unit has been chosen. The *atomic mass unit* was defined as 1/12 of the mass of the carbon isotope with mass 12. Hence carbon-12 (or ^{12}C) has a mass of 12 atomic mass units (AMU) and an atomic mass unit equals 1.6599×10^{-24} gram.

To get an idea of size we note that if one atom of gold has a mass of 3.3×10^{-22} gram and gold has a density of 19.3 g/cm³, the volume of a spherical gold atom is 1.3×10^{-23} cm³ if we correct for the volume occupied by space between the gold atoms (26 percent). The radius of the gold atoms can be estimated from the equation of the volume of a sphere ($4\pi r^3/3$, where r is the radius) to be about 1.4×10^{-8} cm. The quantity 10^{-8} cm is called an *angstrom* (Å); thus the radius of a gold atom is about 1.4 Å.

The atom is actually a "fluffy" sphere mainly because of the low density of the electron clouds. The nucleus is much more dense; its radius is only about 10^{-12} cm, but it contains more than 99.9 percent of the mass of an atom.

There is a small but significant difference between the mass of the proton and the neutron; furthermore, nuclides have masses less than the simple sum of the mass of the constituent nucleons.

These observations can be understood in terms of the famous Einstein equation relating mass and energy:

$$E = mc^2$$

where E is energy, m is mass, and c is the velocity of light. We will rewrite this equation in a more useful form for our purposes:

$$\Delta E = c^2 \, \Delta m$$

where ΔE is the change in energy related through the proportionality constant c^2 to the change in mass, Δm. That is, the difference in mass between the starting materials (nucleons) and the resulting product (the nucleus of the nuclide of interest) is released as energy. We will explore this concept in greater detail.

In atomic dimensions it is useful to define not only a new mass unit but also a unit of energy that can be managed easily. For this purpose the energy unit called an *electron volt* is commonly used. Formally defined, the electron volt is the energy acquired by an electron during its acceleration across a voltage difference of 1 volt. Practically, it is a unit small enough to use easily in calculations involving atomic scale phenomena. An electron volt is equal to 3.88×10^{-20} calorie, a very small quantity when one considers that a teaspoon of sugar supplies 20,000 calories (or 20 Calories – the capital is used by nutritionists to mean 1000 calories) on burning!

For example, the helium isotope ^4He has a mass number of 4 (= the number of nucleons, two protons and two neutrons in the nucleus) but a mass of 4.002604 AMU.

If we take a hypothetical reaction in which we combine four atoms of hydrogen (^1H) each with a mass of 1.007825 AMU to form one atom of helium (^4He), the change in mass will be

$$4 \, ^1\text{H} = \, ^4\text{He}$$

or

$$4 \times (1.007825) = 4.002604 + \Delta m$$

where Δm is the mass not found in the helium atom and is equal to 0.028697 AMU. Using the Einstein equation, the energy equivalent of this mass is 26.6 million electron volts (MeV).

Hence the reaction of four hydrogens to one helium-4 will release about 10^{-12} calorie. The energy derived from 1 gram of hydrogen (1 mole) when "fused" to form helium is then

$$\frac{1}{4} \times 10^{-12} \text{ calorie/atom} \times 6.023 \times 10^{23} \text{ atoms/mole} = 1.5 \times 10^{11} \text{ calories}$$

Of course this reaction is far from hypothetical, since it is the main source of the sun's energy! For comparison, 1 gram of hydrogen "burned" with oxygen to form water yields 3×10^4 calories, or only one five-millionth of the nuclear energy.

From this reaction we can see that about 6 MeV (million electron volts) of energy per nucleon is released. If we form ^{4}He from the constituent nucleons instead of from hydrogen atoms, the resulting mass decrease is expressed as the *binding energy*. The binding energy per nucleon, $\bar{B}$, is determined in the following way:

$$\bar{B} = \frac{[M_p Z + M_n (A - Z) - M] c^2}{A}$$

where M_p and M_n are the masses of the proton and the neutron, M is the mass of the nuclide, A is the mass number of the nuclide, Z is the atomic number of the nuclide, and c is the speed of light.

The binding energy per nucleon varies as a function of mass number, as can be seen in Fig. 1-4. The top of the curve is the region of maximum stability. Here the greatest amount of energy is required to be added per nucleon to disintegrate the nucleus and disperse the constituent nucleons.

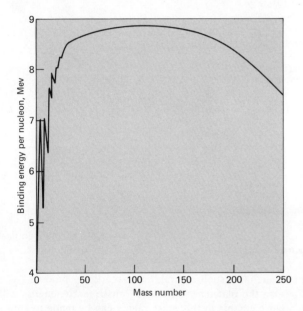

Figure 1-4 Binding energy per nucleon as a function of mass number.

It follows from the foregoing discussion that energy will be released in nuclear reactions as long as the binding energy per nucleon of the aggregate of products is greater than the binding energy per nucleon of the aggregate starting materials.

The reaction in which four hydrogens react to form one helium atom, as we saw, results in a release of energy and a net increase in the binding energy per nucleon of the product (helium) over the starting material (hydrogen). This class of reaction is called *fusion*. Fusion can be brought about only if the force of repulsion of the positively charged atomic nuclei is overcome. Energy must be supplied to the nuclei so that this repulsive force is overcome. The resulting energy release, when fusion occurs, far exceeds the amount of energy supplied to overcome the repulsive force. This is the basis for the hydrogen bomb, the heat production of the stars, and some-day, it is hoped, controlled power production by fusion to meet man's evergrowing energy needs.

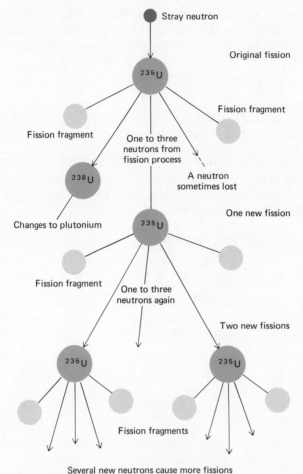

Stray neutron

Original fission

^{235}U

Fission fragment

Fission fragment

One to three
neutrons from
fission process

A neutron
sometimes lost

^{238}U

One new fission

Changes to plutonium

^{235}U

Fission fragment

One to three
neutrons again

Two new fissions

^{235}U

^{235}U

Fission fragments

Several new neutrons cause more fissions

Figure 1-5 Induced fission
of ^{235}U by neutrons.

The high-mass-number nuclides, such as uranium, have lower binding energies per nucleon than nuclides on the plateau in Fig. 1-4. Consequently, energy will be released if uranium or other elements in this mass region can be made to split into nuclides along the plateau. This is called *fission*. For some heavy nuclides this occurs spontaneously, but for others the fissioning can be made to accelerate greatly by bombardment with neutrons (Fig. 1-5). This is the basis of the "atomic" bomb and the many active nuclear reactors used for research and power production.

THE DISTRIBUTION OF ELECTRONS AROUND THE NUCLEUS

We will now consider the configuration of the electrons that revolve, orbitlike, around the nucleus of an atom. The spatial distribution of the electrons is not a random one, as is clear from a variety of evidence. Transformations in the spatial distribution pattern of electrons in an atom results in the emission or absorption of light of distinctive wavelengths (for example, the yellow flame produced by sodium when table salt —

sodium chloride—is put in a flame is composed of a single dominant wavelength, associated with changes in the distribution of electrons in the excited sodium atom). This effect indicates that a distinctive quantity of energy is releasable as though there are discrete jumps from one electronic configuration to another. Also, certain types of chemical bonds (discussed in detail later) require that the atom be "shaped" to give definite angles of attachment to other atoms. These directional bonds require a preferred orientation of the field occupied by some of the electrons, since it is the electron cloud and not the small, protected nucleus that gives an atom its chemical or bonding properties.

The best way to describe the disposition of electrons in atoms is through the language of *quantum mechanics*. Each electron is assigned a characteristic set of quantum numbers—a coded statement about the distribution of that electron around the nucleus. The derivation of the scheme is beyond the scope of this book but the results can be expressed fairly easily.

Four quantum numbers are necessary to describe the characteristics of an orbiting electron. In an atom no two electrons can have the same set of quantum numbers. The first quantum number is called the *principal quantum number* (n); it can assume values of $n = 1, 2, 3, \cdots$. In the early days of atomic theory it was assumed that the orbiting electrons were grouped into a series of concentric "shells." These were designated, from the nucleus outward, $K, L, M, N, \cdots$. The role of the "shell" has been taken over by the principal quantum number in the more precise quantum mechanical language. Hence principal quantum number 1 is equivalent to the K-shell, principal quantum number 2 is equivalent to the L-shell, and so on.

The second quantum number, called the *angular quantum number* (l), describes the "shape" of the electron cloud: spherical shell, dumbbell, and so on (Fig. 1-6). The values of l are restricted to certain ones set by the principal quantum number according to the rule:

$$l = (n-1), (n-2), \cdots, 0$$

The third quantum number, designated m, describes the orientation of the configuration given by the angular quantum number l. That is, if the angular quantum number indicates that the electron cloud has the shape of a dumbbell, the m quantum number identifies the different relative orientations of the dumbbell in space (Fig. 1-6). Since these orientations can be identified with the aid of a magnetic field, m is called the *magnetic quantum number*. The values of m are given as follows for a particular l value:

$$m = l, \cdots, 0, \cdots, -l$$

The fourth quantum number, s, is an intrinsic property of the electron. An electron that is spinning has a magnetic polarity because of its charge. Since it can, in principle, spin either clockwise or counterclockwise, two different magnetic polarities would occur. To describe this in terms of a quantum number an electron is said to have either a $+\frac{1}{2}$ *spin* or a $-\frac{1}{2}$ *spin*. Thus any two electrons orbiting the same nucleus would be permitted to have the three quantum numbers n, l, m the same provided that they have opposite spins. The description of an electron associated with an atom in this manner can be compared with the idea of the electron revolving around the nucleus in some orbit. But the quantum mechanical language is basically probabilistic; hence, rather than describing definite electron orbits, it describes a

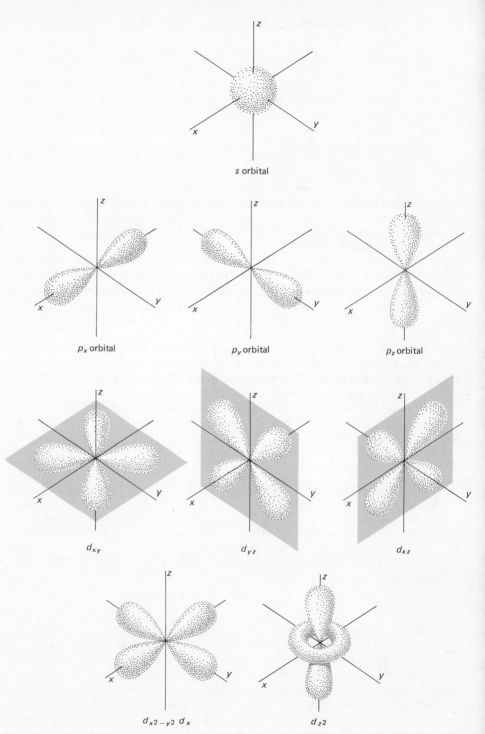

Figure 1-6 Visualizations of some of the configurations represented by different angular quantum numbers.

fuzzy cloud. The quantum number coding is then a description that is called an *orbital* rather than an orbit.

As we have noted at the beginning of this section, quantum mechanics had a strong beginning in the study of the spectral lines associated with energy changes in atoms caused by changes in the electronic configuration. Consequently, a homey nomenclature developed around the description of the l quantum number. It was on the basis of the quality of the spectral lines associated with jumps of electrons from one orbital to another that individual l values were assigned symbolic designations as follows:

	Symbol	Original Meaning
$l = 0$	s	"sharp"
$l = 1$	p	"principal"
$l = 2$	d	"diffuse"
$l = 3$	f	"fundamental"

The original meanings are now almost irrelevant, but the symbols have remained.

THE PERIODIC CHART AND THE AUFBAU PRINCIPLE

The relation of spectral lines to jumps between orbitals also gives an idea about the relative energy levels of each of the orbitals described by the quantum numbers. The lowest energy level orbital can be thought of as being closest to the nucleus. To move the electron out of this orbital to a more "distant" orbital requires energy to overcome the attractive force of the nucleus; hence it is said that a higher energy level is attained.

The lowest energy level orbital associated with any particular principal quantum number is the s orbital. The progressively higher energy level orbitals are in the order p, d, f, $\cdots$ (as permitted by the principal quantum number). It can also be shown that, proceeding from the K-shell ($n = 1$) to more and more remote "shells" from the nucleus, the energy level also increases. A single electron will occupy the $n = 1$ shell first, and only with increasing energy input will move up to $n = 2$, and so forth.

The relationships between the elements were established on the basis of chemical affinities among groups of elements. This resulted in the familiar periodic chart shown in Fig. 1-7. We can now use our model of orbitals to understand the atomic basis of the periodic chart. If we undertake the project of proceeding through the periodic chart of the elements by adding successively one proton after another to the nucleus (with the necessary number of neutrons to get a stable nucleus) we will also have to add electrons to maintain electrical neutrality. The electrons are added to orbitals as described above. Each electron will occupy the lowest possible energy level as it is added with the constraint that no two electrons can have the identical four quantum numbers. The concept of building up the periodic chart by adding electrons as the proton number increases is called the *Aufbau principle*. (*Aufbau* is the German word for "building up.")

Figure 1-8 shows the energy levels of the orbitals. Each electron added will occupy the lowest energy orbital that is available to it. Hence the first electron will occupy a $1s$ orbital. The addition of another electron to the $1s$ orbital will be possible

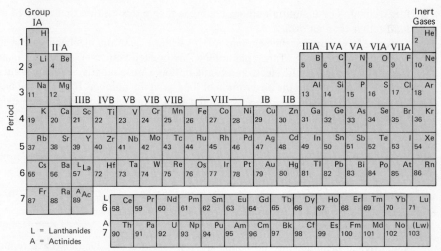

Figure 1-7   The periodic chart of the elements.

if the spin of the added electron is opposite to that already occupying the orbital. Two 1s electrons with opposite spins balancing the nuclear charge describes the element helium. There are no other orbitals possible for a principal quantum number $n = 1$; hence helium is a "closed shell" atom. The closed or completed shell is correlated with a chemical inertness.

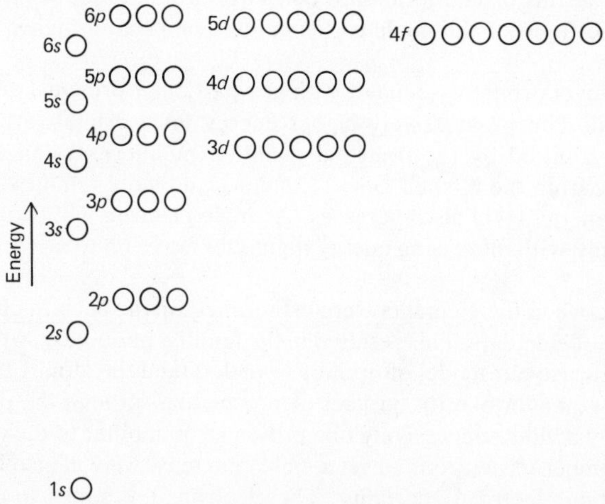

Figure 1-8   The stability sequence of orbitals.

The third electron will go into the 2s orbital, forming lithium, and the fourth will also go into the 2s orbital with opposite spin, to form beryllium. By this process the periodic chart of Fig. 1-7 is filled out (Table 1-1).

Reference

GAMOW, G., *Matter, Earth, and Sky*. Englewood Cliffs, New Jersey. Prentice Hall, 1958, 593 pp. (also in paperback).

2 The Abundance and the Origin of the Elements

We have seen that the chemical elements can be systematized both in terms of their nuclear properties and their chemical properties. Our next inquiry is logically into what the mechanisms of formation of the elements were and what factors control their distribution in the universe. In order to answer these questions we must turn to the solar system and beyond, since on earth we are restricted to a superficial sampling of the uppermost part of the earth's crust – a sampling hardly representative of the whole earth, much less of the solar system or the universe. Our most direct insight comes from the study of sunlight and from the only members of the solar system (aside from the earth) for which we have an extensive sampling – the meteorites.

METEORITES

Meteorites are pieces of stone and iron that fall from the sky. They are to be distinguished from *meteors,* which are the trails made by the disintegration of particles entering our atmosphere, most of which never reach the earth's surface in recognizable form. Very bright meteors, called "fireballs," often terminate as recoverable meteorites.

Such a fireball, traveling from north to south across New England on December 14, 1807, exploded over Weston, Connecticut. Several pieces of this, the first meteorite seen to fall by the non-Indian residents of America, were recovered and are preserved in museums (Fig. 2-1).

The thought of stones and irons falling from the sky was revolutionary even to as progressive and informed a man as President Thomas Jefferson during whose administration the Weston meteorite was observed to fall. He wrote down his skepticism in a letter to one of the possessors of the meteorite fragments who had asked him to present the meteorite to Congress for examination and certification. After suggesting that a scientific rather than a legislative body might best make scientific judgments, Jefferson wrote:

We certainly are not to deny whatever we cannot account for. A thousand phenomena present themselves daily which we cannot explain, but where facts are

25 cm

Figure 2-1 Weston Meteorite.

suggested, bearing no analogy with the laws of nature as yet known to us, their verity needs proofs proportional to their difficulty. A cautious mind will weigh well the opposition of the phenomenon to everything hitherto observed, the strength of the testimony by which it is supported and the errors and misconceptions to which even our senses are liable. It may be difficult to explain how the stone you possess came into the position in which it was found. But is it easier to explain how it got into the clouds from whence it is supposed to have fallen?

This was not a particularly uncommon response of learned men in the New World. Indeed, the recovery of a meteorite actually seen to fall at L'Aigle in France a few years earlier had begun the controversy in Europe. The beginning of the nineteenth century thus saw the beginning of the study of meteorites, as well as of many other scientific pursuits. Althought it is true that other meteorites had been seen to fall before this time, the reports were generally rejected in the Age of Reason as legendary or mythical.

Most meteorites, like the Weston meteorite, enter the earth's atmosphere with sufficiently low momentum because of their small size (about 1 metric ton, or 1 million grams, for a good-sized stone meteorite), eventually to reach a relatively low velocity, dictated by atmospheric friction, similar to that of a parcel falling from a high-flying airplane. These meteorites are warm when recovered, but not red-hot. Indeed the interiors often are ice-cold.

A smaller number of meteorites come at the earth with such high momentum, because of their great mass and velocity, that they penetrate the atmosphere and impact with tremendous force and produce explosion craters. Some of the meteorite and the rock it impacts is volatilized and the rest strewn around the point of impact. High-pressure minerals such as coesite in the rock (a form of silicon dioxide) and diamonds in the meteorite fragments are formed by the impact. A typical explosion crater produced by this method is the Meteor Crater in Winslow, Arizona (Fig. 2-2) with which the Canyon Diablo iron meteorites are associated. The total recovered mass of the meteorite is 20 metric tons but it has been shown that this crater with a 1200-meter (4000-foot) diameter was formed in prehistoric times by the impact of a

Figure 2-2   Meteor Crater, Arizona. Spence Air Photo.

mass weighing 60,000 metric tons. Much of the material was dispersed as very fine-grained debris.

Meteorites are classified into stones, irons, and stony irons. The stones are not easily distinguished when seen in association with terrestrial rocks unless specifically sought; hence, most of the stony meteorites in museums were recovered only because they were actually observed to fall. The irons and stony irons, on the other hand, are so unlike any terrestrial rock that meteorites of these types lying on the surface of the earth appear highly distinctive even thousands of years after they fell.

The stones are easily classified further into two major types. By far the largest number of stones are of the type called *chondrites* because they commonly contain small spherical *chondrules* (from the Greek meaning a "grain") about 1mm in diameter (Fig. 2-3).

Both the chondrules and the rest of the material of chondrites are composed of constituents typical of those in basalt, a volcanic rock abundant in the Hawaiian Islands and elsewhere. It is believed by some meteorite experts that the presence of chondrules may be explained as a product of volcanic activity on a planetary body that formed from the solar nebula and then broke up; others believe that condensation from a primitive solar nebula could have produced spherical droplets directly. Metallic iron is finely dispersed throughout the chondritic meteorites, causing the density of most chondrites to be considerably above that of any terrestrial rock. The overall chemical composition of chondrites is remarkably constant. One class of chondrites, the *carbonaceous chondrites,* differ from the others in having up to 5 percent organic carbon and 20 percent of water tied up in compounds.

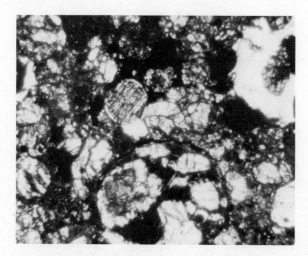

Figure 2-3 Photomicrograph of Weston meteorite showing a chondrule.

The second group of stone meteorites contains no chondrules and hence is called the *achondritic* group. Achondrites are fewer and have highly variable compositions.

The iron meteorites (Fig. 2-4) are composed of two alloys of iron and nickel with blebs of iron sulfide called *troilite*. When an iron meteorite is sliced and polished and the surface is etched by acid, the two alloys dissolve in the acid at different rates, producing a marked relief pattern called the *Widmanstätten figure*. The pattern is the result of the slow migration of nickel and iron after the iron was a solid to form a nickel-poor alloy, *kamacite,* from an originally homogeneous alloy of iron-nickel called *taenite*. The width of the bands is dictated by the nickel content of the whole meteorite (the lower the nickel content, the wider the bands). The original solid iron masses were parts of larger bodies, perhaps 100 km in diameter. In bodies of this size the rate of cooling is slow: about 1–2°C per million years. This slow cooling permitted the migration of the nickel and iron atoms in the solid to produce the two alloys making up the Widmanstätten figure.

ABUNDANCES OF THE ELEMENTS IN THE SOLAR SYSTEM

Meteorites are studied for what they tell us about the chemical composition of planetary material and the solar system. This composition provides clues to the origin of the chemical elements and their distribution among the planets and the sun. It is obvious that we cannot use the composition of rocks on the surface of the earth for the solar system as a whole, because the earth's crust is the complex product of many years of modification by the processes acting peculiarly in the outer shell of the earth. Probably the most representative sample is the sun. Sunlight gives prime information on the composition of the sun's outer layers, which are probably least affected by the continuing thermonuclear reactions of the sun's interior, as discussed later in this chapter. Two difficulties are inherent in estimates of solar system elemental abundances based on the solar spectrum. One is that the conversion factors between spectral-line properties and elemental abundances are not precisely known for some elements and the other is that the abundances of some elements are too low in relation to their spectral sensitivity to permit detection.

Figure 2-4 (a) An iron meteorite being cut. This is the 20-metric-ton Cape York meteorite from Greenland recently recovered by Dr. Vagn Buchwald and transported to Denmark for processing. The slab is 180 cm by 130 cm and 5 cm thick. The round blebs are iron sulfide ("troilite"). Courtesy of Dr. Vagn Buchwald. See also V. F. Buchwald, *Meteoritics,* **6,** 27 (1971).

Chondritic meteorites are reasonably homogeneous in composition for many elements, and where comparison is possible with solar spectral data the relative concentrations of the elements are similar. As a first approximation, then, the composition of chondritic meteorites gives the original composition of matter in the solar system except for the volatile elements. The latter include not only hydrogen, carbon, nitrogen, and oxygen, but also the rare gases and certain particularly "volatile" metals such as mercury, thallium, bismuth, and lead. High concentrations of the "volatile" metals are preserved, however, in the carbonaceous chondrites described earlier. The organic compounds and the high water content of the solids indicate a low temperature of accumulation of the material in these meteorites. This also permitted the retention of the volatile metals although the gases like hydrogen would be mainly lost. With the data thus obtained (Table 2-1), we can proceed to ask what processes lead to the synthesis of elements in the galaxy.

THE ORIGIN OF THE ELEMENTS

We have seen in the previous section that the dominant element in the sun is hydrogen, with helium running a close second. This picture is the same for all the stars in our galaxy and in other galaxies as well.

Figure 2-4   (b) An etched slab of another iron meteorite, Gibeon, showing the two alloys taenite and kamacite forming the Widmanstätten figures. This is revealed by acid etching. The round bleb is iron sulfide ("troilite").

Although the helium content of the universe may in large part be due to its earliest stage of evolution, it is generally agreed that some of the helium and all the other elements began with the simplest nuclide, hydrogen ^{1}H.

Stars are the main factories for the manufacture of the elements. Although the details are far from completely known, enough has been learned in the past 15 years to make a reasonable guess at the pathways of element formation. The formation of the elements (more precisely, the nuclides) is called *nucleosynthesis*.

Nuclear Reactions

Theories of nucleosynthesis are based on nuclear reactions observed in the laboratory or reasonably projected from nuclear theory and on observations of different types of stars and their properties. What the alchemists could not attain—the transformation of one element to another—has become the everyday expectancy of nuclear scientists. It is the knowledge of these transformations that has led to fruitful theories of the origin of the elements. Before looking at the general scheme for the formation of the elements we must acquaint ourselves with some of the rudimentary aspects of nuclear reactions.

A nucleus that is unstable will change spontaneously and, in the process, emit energy in the form of radiation. It is thus said to be *radioactive*.

The earliest radioactive nuclides studied were those in the uranium and thorium radioactivity series, including the element radium. Three types of radiation being emitted by these radioactive nuclides (Fig. 2-5) were identified: the α particle (a ^{4}He nucleus unaccompanied by electrons), the β^- particle (a fast moving electron),

Table 2-1 Comparisons of Solar, Meteoritic and "Cosmic" abundances[a]

	Sun	Carbonaceous Chondrites	"Cosmic" (Cameron)
H	4.8×10^{10}	5.5×10^6	2.6×10^{10}
Li	1.7	50	45
Be	11	0.81	0.69
C	1.7×10^7	8.2×10^5	1.35×10^7
N	4.6×10^6	4.9×10^4	2.44×10^6
O	4.4×10^7	7.7×10^6	2.36×10^7
Na	9.1×10^4	6.0×10^4	6.32×10^4
Mg	7.4×10^5	1.07×10^6	1.050×10^6
Al	6.9×10^4	8.5×10^4	8.51×10^4
Si	$\equiv1.0\times10^6$	$\equiv1.0\times10^6$	$\equiv1.0\times10^6$
P	1.9×10^4	1.27×10^4	1.27×10^4
S	8.0×10^5	5.1×10^5	5.06×10^5
K	2,200	3,200	3,240
Ca	6.0×10^4	7.2×10^4	7.36×10^4
Sc	30	31	33
Ti	1,800	2,300	2,300
V	630	298	900
Cr	3,800	1.27×10^4	1.24×10^4
Mn	3,000	9,300	8,800
Fe	2.5×10^5	9.0×10^5	8.90×10^5
Co	2,400	2,200	2,300
Ni	2.3×10^4	4.9×10^4	4.57×10^4
Cu	160	590	919
Zn	250	1,500	1,500
Ga	20	46	45.5
Ge	16	130	126
Rb	10	6.0	5.95
Sr	25	24	58.4
Y	80(?)	4.6	4.6
Zr	20	32	30
Nb	10	—	1.15
Mo	10	—	2.52
Ru	3	1.85	1.6
Rh	1	—	0.33
Pd	1	1.28	1.5
Ag	0.4	0.95	0.5
Cd	3	2.1	2.12
In	1	0.22	0.217
Sn	6(?)	4.2	4.22
Sb	0.1(?)	0.40	0.381
Ba	16	4.7	4.7
Yb	8(?)	0.21	0.21
Pb	4	2.9	2.90

[a]After G. Goles, *Handbook of Geochemistry* (Springer-Verlag, 1969).

and the γ ray (electromagnetic radiation of shorter wavelength than visible light, ultraviolet light, or X rays).

Further studies showed that in some cases a positron or β^+ particle — similar to a β^- particle in mass but exactly opposite in charge — may be emitted. In still another style of decay, an electron from the inner shell of orbiting electrons may be captured by the nucleus.

Let us look at the "reactions" and the products formed by these different modes of radioactivity. Remembering that A is used as the symbol for mass number and Z for the proton number, we construct the following table.

Particle Emitted	Original Radioactive Nuclide ("parent")	Resulting Nuclide ("daughter")
α	Z, A	$Z - 2, A - 4$
β^-	Z, A	$Z + 1, A$
γ	Z, A	$Z,\quad A$
β^+	Z, A	$Z - 1, A$
Electron capture	Z, A	$Z - 1, A$

With every β^- or β^+ decay, additional energy is released from the nucleus in the form of a *neutrino* which carries energy but interacts with matter so poorly that only the most sensitive techniques can be used to see it. The story of the neutrino is a good example of a particle that had to be "invented" to satisfy the demands of theory, and whose actual existence was subsequently vindicated.

We can also use various nuclear and subnuclear projectiles to modify the nucleus. These projectiles have become easily available in nuclear reactors and accelerators that are the "grandchildren" of the cyclotron. *Cosmic rays* (exceedingly energetic nuclei and subnuclear particles arriving from space) are a natural source of projectiles that can produce certain nuclear transformations. An example is the production of carbon-14 in the atmosphere from nitrogen-14. Carbon-14 is radioactive, and slowly, at its characteristic rate, returns to nitrogen-14. Its rate of transformation has been used for dating certain types of carbon-containing archaeological artifacts (see Chapter 7). Let us follow the sequence of reactions in the carbon-14 production and decay cycle.

Protons make up the major part of cosmic rays and have energies of *billions* of electronvolts. These proton projectiles smash into nitrogen nuclei (^{14}N primarily) at very high altitudes in our atmosphere and "spall" off a variety of products including neutrons with masses smaller than the original nucleus. The energies of the newly produced neutrons are very great but after many collisions with the atoms in the air the neutrons become thermalized by the time they reach about 15 kilometers above the earth's surface; that is, they have energies of motion characteristic of particles in a low-temperature gas. The reaction of the low-energy neutron with ^{14}N results in the formation of ^{14}C and a proton. This is written in shorthand:

$$^{14}N(n, p)^{14}C$$

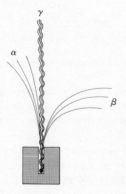

Figure 2-5 The three types of radiation emitted from radium as discriminated by a magnetic field.

which reads: "to a ^{14}N nucleus a neutron (n) is added and a proton (p) is ejected, resulting in a ^{14}C nucleus."

Other reactions involving neutrons have been performed in nuclear reactors where large fluxes of neutrons are produced. For instance if we put ^{59}Co (the only stable isotope of cobalt) into a reactor and bombard it with neutrons, a reaction of neutron capture promptly followed by gamma-ray emission will occur. In our shorthand,

$$^{59}\text{Co}(n, \gamma)^{60}\text{Co}$$

which reads: "to a ^{59}Co nucleus a neutron (n) is added and a gamma (γ) ray ejected, resulting in a ^{60}Co nucleus." We will use this shorthand frequently in the following pages to denote the reactions involving the formation of the elements.

The Recipe

The process of nucleosynthesis has been described as a sort of "cosmic cookery" in which a pinch of this nuclear process and a pinch of that are combined to give the observed array of elemental abundances. The fundamental steps of this process spelled out in recipe form are the following:

1. Start with hydrogen primarily (mixed with 25 percent helium).
2. Condense the hydrogen gas into protostars that heat up because of gravitational contraction. A mixture of products from previous stellar events found as debris in the galaxy is also presumed to condense with the hydrogen.
3. At a high enough temperature, commence fusion reactions of hydrogen to form helium and, in the process, light up the star.
4. Continue in successive fusion reactions to the top of the binding-energy curve (at about iron-56).
5. After the formation of the nuclides at the top of the binding-energy curve, form the higher mass nuclides by neutron capture and radioactive decay.

We will now look more closely at the nucleosynthetic scheme outlined briefly above.

Hydrogen Burning

The main fuel of stars is hydrogen. Depending on the mass of the star and on what nuclides have been trapped during its condensation, a number of different ways of "burning" hydrogen (in a nuclear sense) to form helium are possible. Several different paths are shown in Fig. 2-6. The net reaction is as discussed above: four hydrogens fuse to form a helium atom. Since we are climbing up the binding-energy curve, energy is given off and the star is radiant. The reaction is said to be *exothermic*.

The reactions proceed at the center of the star where matter is hottest and densest. During hydrogen burning in the core of a star such as our sun, the density is about 100 g/cm^3 and the temperature is about 17×10^6°K. (°K stands for "degrees Kelvin," or absolute temperature; on the scale 0°C is 273°K, and each degree is the same size as in the centigrade scale. When we are dealing with such high temperatures the difference between the two scales is small, but for consistency we will continue to refer

Process 1:
Direct hydrogen burning

$^1H(p, \beta^+)^2D$

$^2D(p, \gamma)^3He$

$^3He(^3He, 2p)^4He$

Process 2:
Carbon-nitrogen cycle

$^{12}C(p, \gamma)^{13}N$

$^{13}N - \beta^+ \rightarrow ^{13}C$

$^{13}C(p, \gamma)^{14}N$

$^{14}N(p, \gamma)^{15}O$

$^{15}O - \beta^+ \rightarrow ^{15}N$

$^{15}N(p, \alpha)^{12}C$

Figure 2-6 Hydrogen-burning paths. Process 1 is the direct hydrogen burning path. Process 2 utilizes reactions involving ^{12}C.

to the Kelvin scale). The time scale for hydrogen burning can be greater than 5 billion years since our sun has existed that long.

Helium Burning

Eventually, in the core of the star, helium will have increased at the expense of hydrogen and the following series of events will then transpire. First, the heat production in the core is diminished as the hydrogen is used up. The outer envelope of the star expands to retain more heat more effectively. Because by this time the star is large and radiating energy at a lower surface temperature, it appears reddish and is called a *red giant*.

The core collapses during the red giant stage, permitting the shell around the core to become hot enough to continue the hydrogen-burning process, while the core becomes considerably hotter as a result of the release of additional gravitational energy during the collapse. This increased heat energy imparted to the ^4He allows these positively charged nuclei to overcome their mutual repulsion and undergo additional exothermic fusion reactions to form carbon-12:

$$3 \ ^4He \rightarrow \ ^{12}C \ (activated) \rightarrow \ ^{12}C + gamma \ ray$$

To ignite this reaction the density at the core will have to be 100,000 g/cm^3 and the temperature about $10^{8\circ}$K. The time scale of helium burning is much shorter than hydrogen burning—about 10^7 to 10^8 years. During the red giant stage some of the ^{12}C is transformed by interaction with more helium nuclei to form ^{16}O.

Carbon and Oxygen Burning

The next step involves the fusion of ^{12}C and ^{16}O with each other to produce nuclides in the vicinity of ^{28}Si. The production of alphas, protons, and neutrons from these nuclides as the temperature is raised results in nuclear reactions with ^{12}C and ^{16}O, and the nuclides between ^{12}C and ^{28}Si are produced. As the ^{12}C and ^{16}O "burn" they do so explosively, resulting in a *supernova*. Supernovae are stars that suddenly become bright because of some rapid energy production in their cores, with the result that the stars disinegrate. (To ancient astronomers these appeared like the birth of new stars; hence they were called "novae" from the Latin word for "new"—or for very large events, "supernovae.")

In high-density stars the burning of the ^{12}C and ^{16}O can go almost to completion, and the explosive burning of ^{28}Si will follow. By this process, nuclides higher up the binding-energy curve will be produced. In particular, as the temperature approaches $4 \times 10^{9}°K$ ^{56}Ni will finally be produced which on β^- decay will become stable ^{56}Fe. Less abundant neighboring nuclides will also be produced. We have reached the top of the binding-energy curve.

Neutron Capture on the Slow Time Scale (the "s-Process")

A star can shine only as reactions continue in its interior. However, any reactions in which nuclides beyond the top of the binding-energy curve are fused are energy users *(endothermic)* and will not proceed spontaneously.

While the events portrayed above are going on, side reactions involving the production and capture of neutrons are also occurring. Neutrons can be produced in a slow, steady fashion in the red giant stage and, as discussed above, also just prior to the supernova stage. If a star has been accumulated from previously processed galactic debris containing nuclides up to and including ^{56}Fe, a set of secondary reactions will occur. For instance, near the end of helium burning, ^{12}C that has been produced can react with hydrogen injected into the core in flashes from the outer shell and form ^{13}C, in a manner similar to the process shown in Fig. 2-6. The ^{13}C can then react to produce neutrons in the following way:

$$^{13}C \ (\alpha, \ n)^{16}O$$

There are some other schemes to produce neutrons in a slow, continuous flux inside stars.

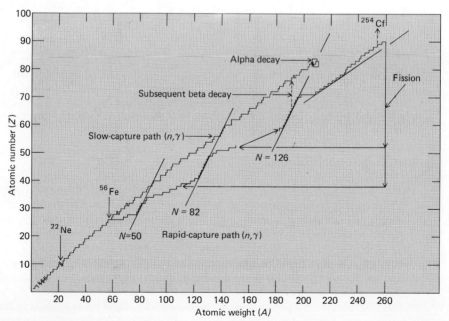

Figure 2-7 Neutron capture on the slow time scale. From G. Burbidge and M. Burbidge, *Science,* **128,** 395 (1958).

The neutron energies are dictated by the temperature of the star, and hence are in essence the energy of motion of gas particles at about 10^8°K just outside the core. The nuclides present just outside the core (particularly ^{56}Fe) are then subject to bombardment by these neutrons, with a time interval between successive neutron capture of 1 to 1×10^5 years. This rate is sufficiently slow to allow most radioactive nuclei—made so by the intrusion of the neutron—to attain stability by β^- radioactive decay. The new, stable nuclide, now of higher mass number, is then bombarded with another neutron and so on until nuclides about as heavy as lead are produced (Fig. 2-7).

The relative abundance of each nuclide depends on how much heavier it is than the "seed" nucleus (^{56}Fe) and upon the stability of the nucleus to further neutron capture. The more reluctant a nuclide is to capture a neutron, the greater its abundance will be. A nucleus may be treated by a mathematical model that likens it to a target, and hence the probability of capturing a neutron is called a *cross section*. A large cross section for neutron capture means this probability is high.

A test of the model implied by the *s*-process is to compare data on experimentally determined neutron capture cross sections with the abundances of nuclides that participate in these reactions. The test then is that a plot of the product of capture cross section (σ) and abundance (N) should decrease continuously with mass number. Such a plot (Fig. 2-8) strongly indicates the validity of this model.

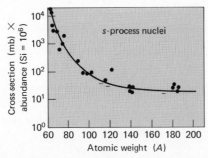 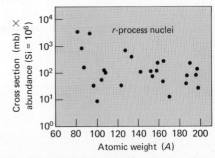

Figure 2-8   The product of neutron capture cross section (σ) and abundance (N) plotted against mass number for nuclides produced by the *s*-process with a comparison to *r*-process nuclides. From J. H. Gibbons and R. L. Macklin, *Science,* **156,** 1039 (1967). Copyright 1967 by the American Association for the Advancement of Science.

Neutron Capture on the Rapid Time Scale (the "*r*-Process")

Many heavy nuclides cannot be produced by the *s*-process. They are the neutron-rich nuclides. Their creation requires the penetration of several neutrons into the nucleus in very rapid succession. The most suitable stellar candidates for the production of such large fluxes appear to be the "neutron" stars, which are produced by the implosion (inward collapse) of the cores of certain stars in which the fuel became exhausted. Unusual neutron-rich seed nuclei, such as ^{78}Ni, may be formed; these nuclei are subsequently bombarded with the large flux of neutrons to produce excess-neutron nuclides all the way up possibly to mass number 298.

A few additional types of nuclear reactions—all of them demonstrated in the laboratory—are required to generate the complexion and abundance of nuclides we see in the sun and meteorites. Exact stellar models for these processes are less certain.

References

BURBIDGE, M., and G. BURBIDGE, "Formation of Elements in the Stars," *Science,* **128,** 387–399, 1958.

CAMERON, A. G. W., *The Structure of the Universe* (to be published) New York: Holt, Rinehart and Winston.

FOWLER, W. A., "The Origin of the Elements," *Chemical and Engineering News,* March 16, p. 90–104, 1964.

FRIEDLANDER, G., J. W. KENNEDY, and J. M. MILLER, *Nuclear and Radioactivity.* New York: John Wiley & Sons, 1964, 585 pp. (2nd ed.).

MASON, B., *Meteorites.* New York: John Wiley & Sons, 1962, 274 pp.

WOOD, J. A., "Meteorites and the Origin of Planets," *Earth and Planetary Science Series* (P. M. Hurley, consulting ed.). New York: McGraw-Hill, 1968, 117 pp.

3 The Chemical Bond

Except for the so-called noble gases (helium, neon, argon, krypton, xenon, and radon), none of the elements exist as single, isolated atoms. The atoms form *chemical bonds* with atoms of their own kind or different kinds. For example, oxygen in the atmosphere exists primarily as O_2; that is, two oxygens are firmly attached together to form a *molecule*. Sodium occurs commonly in nature as sodium chloride (NaCl); that is, household table salt. The number of sodium and chlorine atoms forming the arrangement visible to the eye as small cubes are of the order of 10^{20} or more atoms. They are attached together in an orderly fashion to form a *crystal*. Similarly, gold (Au) appearing as a shiny metal is the result of gold atoms bound together in a regular arrangement to form a cohesive crystalline material.

The chemical bond between atoms is the most important aspect of matter in describing its chemical qualities. From the examples given above and others like them, scientists have resolved the forces binding atoms together into five major types. They are: ionic bonding, covalent bonding, metallic bonding, hydrogen bonding, and bonding through van der Waals forces. In reality a compound or molecule must nearly always be described as featuring two or more of these basic idealized bond types.

In order to transform these words into lively concepts, we must return to the discussion of the periodic chart and the Aufbau principle in Chapter 1, and to our experience about the chemical inertness of the noble gases. The noble gases are characterized by "closed shells," that is, s and p orbitals are filled and the next highest energy level to be filled when an electron is added is an s orbital (see Table 1-1). We must thus presume that there is a correlation between closed shells and chemical stability or inertness.

On the basis of the chemical inertness of the noble gases, we are led to postulate that the atoms of all the other elements will be in their most stable states if their electronic configurations simulate the closed-shell noble-gas configuration. This can be done only by gaining or losing the appropriate number of electrons. The different types of bonding are essentially nature's solutions to this problem.

COVALENT BONDING

Let us again consider the example of oxygen. The atom has an atomic number (Z) of 8, with the following electronic structure: two electrons in $1s$, two electrons in $2s$, two electrons in $2p_x$, and one electron each in $2p_y$ and $2p_z$. In order to take on the neon-gas configuration (the closest noble gas), each oxygen must in principle complete its $2p_y$ and $2p_z$ orbitals by adding an electron to each. This effect can be accomplished if two oxygen atoms come together and share $2p_y$ and $2p_z$ orbitals. This way, each atom will appear to itself to have filled these orbitals at least half the time statistically, and the bond will add stability to the oxygen atom.

The sharing of electrons results in *covalent bonds*. Other common examples of covalently bonded compounds are water (H_2O) and methane (CH_4). The nature of the covalent bond is to share electrons. Since orbitals assume only certain orientations in space, the covalent bonds also form with these orientations.

In the case of water, $1s$ orbitals (spherical distribution) of two hydrogens, each containing only one electron, are each attached to one of the singly occupied $2p$ orbitals of oxygen. Ordinarily, the p orbitals are in the form of dumbbells at right angles to each other, but in H_2O the angle of 90° is increased to 103° because the two identically charged hydrogen nuclei tend to repel each other (Fig. 3-1). This is a simple explanation using the orbitals as we have defined them. A better understanding of the water molecule can be attained by the procedures described below.

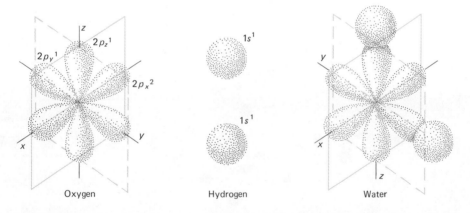

Figure 3-1 Covalent bonding in the water molecule. Oxygen has two incomplete $2p$ orbitals and the $1s$ hydrogen orbital has only one electron. By covalent bonding the $1s$ orbitals of two hydrogens combine with the $2p_x$ and $2p_y$ orbitals to form the water molecule. The angle between the hydrogen atoms is actually 103° instead of 90° because of the mutual repulsion of the two similarly charged hydrogen nuclei.

This model has proved so useful in understanding the directional properties of covalent bonding that it has been extended by the construction of additional geometries than the basic ones given in Fig. 1-6. An association of covalently bonded atoms often reaches a lower energy state (the ideal is always to lower the energy state of the molecule just as it is in an atom) if the original orbitals of one or both of the combining atoms are each merged or blended into *hybrid* orbitals. This operation

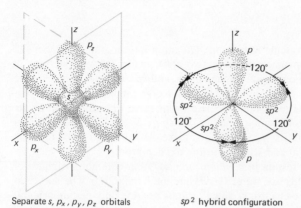 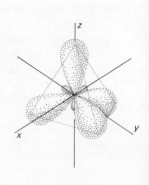

Separate s, p_x, p_y, p_z orbitals sp^2 hybrid configuration sp^3 hybrid orbitals

Figure 3-2 Hybridization of s and p orbitals.

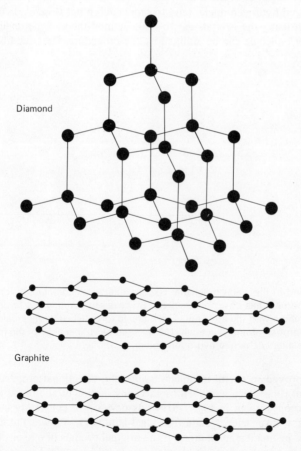

Diamond

Graphite

Figure 3-3 Comparison of the structure of graphite and diamond.

explains the observed directional properties of covalent bonds, especially in organic compounds, which are otherwise not easy to comprehend. We shall draw our examples of hybrid orbitals from minerals.

Graphite and Diamond

Polymorphs are different atomic arrangements of the same atoms, yielding solids with totally different properties. Carbon is a particularly suitable example because two common polymorphs, graphite and diamond, form covalent bonds exclusively.

The unhybridized electron distribution in the carbon atom is

$$1s^2 \; 2s^2 \; 2p_x{}^1 \; 2p_y{}^1$$

(The superscripts refer to the number of electrons — one or two — in an orbital. A completely vacant orbital is not listed.) Strongly bound sheets of carbon atoms held loosely to other sheets give graphite its slippery or lubricating qualities. How can we rationalize such properties by hybridizing the orbitals? The answer is shown in Fig. 3-2. Each $2sp^2$ orbital is a hybrid of a $2s$, a $2p_x$, and a $2p_z$ orbital, which form three lobes in the x-z plane 120° apart. Perpendicular to this plane is the unhybridized $2p_y$ orbital. Each hybridized and unhybridized orbital has one electron, an improvement over leaving one $2p$ orbital completely vacant as far as bonding is concerned. The graphite structure develops as shown in Fig. 3-3 in order to bring to two the number of electrons in each orbital.

The other polymorph of carbon, diamond, is the hardest mineral known to man and does not have preferred planes of slippage. Graphite is used as a lubricant, whereas diamond is used as an abrasive.

To form the structure of diamond, we take the four electrons in the $2s$ and $2p$ orbitals and we construct four identical orbitals, each having one part $2s$ and three parts $2p$. This new hybrid orbital is called the $2sp^3$ orbital. Four equal orbitals each occupied by a single electron will form a tetrahedron as seen in Fig. 3-2. Bonding by overlap of adjacent $2sp^3$ orbitals produces a three-dimensional array of carbon atoms with the great strength of diamond (Fig. 3-3).

Covalent Bonding in Radicals

Covalent bonding may also be found in smaller discrete units called *radicals:* sulfate ($SO_4{}^{-2}$), carbonate ($CO_3{}^{-2}$), phosphate ($PO_4{}^{-3}$), and others (Fig. 3-4). Radicals behave as cohesive units, whether they are found in solution or as parts of solids.

In the carbonate radical, the $2sp^2$ hybridized orbitals of the carbon atom all are in a plane (as in graphite) and each of these orbitals is overlapped by one of the $2p$ orbitals of each of three oxygens. The unhybridized $2p_y$ electron is "stolen" from the carbon atom and used to fill the single unpaired orbital in one of the three oxygens, and two additional electrons are taken from the environment to complete the same requirements of the other oxygen atoms. This leaves the carbonate radical doubly negatively charged, and thus it is written $CO_3{}^{-2}$.

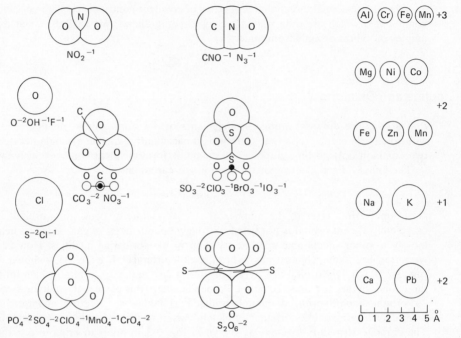

Figure 3-4   Relative sizes of atoms, ions, and "radicals."

IONIC BONDING

Another way to attain a noble-gas electronic configuration is by complete capture or complete release of electrons. The resulting charged species is called an *ion*. The CO_3^{-2} radical was made, for example, by capturing two electrons, as discussed above; hence it is an ion. An element that releases electrons very easily is said to be *electropositive*, and an element that attracts an electron strongly is *electronegative*. An atom that has lost one or more electrons is positively charged; such an ion in solution would be attracted to a negatively charged "cathode," and hence is called a *cation*. Conversely, an ion that has gained electrons would be attracted to a positively charged "anode," so it is called an *anion*.

Sodium Chloride

We return to the case of sodium chloride mentioned at the beginning of this chapter. The sodium electronic structure is

$$1s^2\ 2s^2\ 2p_x^2\ 2p_y^2\ 2p_z^2\ 3s^1$$

To attain the neon configuration (the "nearest" noble gas) it must lose the $3s$ electron. The chlorine electronic structure is

$$1s^2\ 2s^2\ 2p_x^2\ 2p_y^2\ 2p_z^2\ 3s^2\ 3p_x^2\ 3p_y^2\ 3p_z^1$$

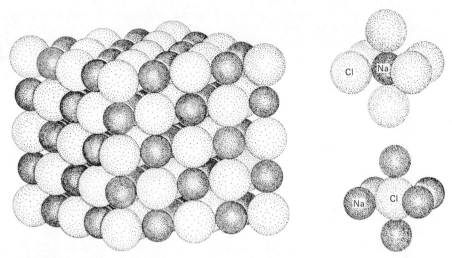

Figure 3-5 Packing of ions as shown by the sodium chloride structure.

Table 3-1 Ionic Radii of Some Common Ions

Element	Oxidation State	Radius (angstroms)	Element	Oxidation State	Radius (angstroms)
Aluminum	+3	0.50	Magnesium	+2	0.65
Antimony	+5	0.62	Manganese	+2	0.80
	+3	0.90		+3	0.66
Arsenic	+5	0.47		+4	0.54
	+3	0.69	Mercury	+2	1.10
Barium	+2	1.35	Molybdenum	+4	0.67
Beryllium	+2	0.31		+6	0.62
Bismuth	+5	0.74	Nickel	+2	0.72
	+3	1.20	Nitrogen	−3	1.71
Boron	+3	0.20	Oxygen	−2	1.40
Bromine	−1	1.95	Potassium	+1	1.33
Cadmium	+2	0.97	Rubidium	+1	1.48
Calcium	+2	0.99	Selenium	−2	1.98
Carbon	+4	0.15	Silicon	+4	0.41
Cesium	+1	1.69	Silver	+1	1.26
Chlorine	−1	1.81	Sodium	+1	0.95
Chromium	+2	0.84	Strontium	+2	1.13
	+3	0.69	Sulfur	−2	1.84
	+6	0.52	Tellurium	−2	2.21
Cobalt	+2	0.74	Thallium	+3	0.95
Copper	+1	0.96		+1	1.40
Fluorine	−1	1.36	Thorium	+4	1.06
Gallium	+3	0.62	Tin	+4	0.71
Gold	+1	1.37		+2	1.12
Hydroxyl (OH^{-1})	−1	1.40	Titanium	+4	0.68
Indium	+3	0.81		+3	0.76
Iodine	−1	2.16		+2	0.90
Iron	+2	0.76	Tungsten	+6	0.67
	+3	0.64	Uranium	+4	0.97
Lead	+2	1.20	Vanadium	+4	0.60
	+4	0.84	Zinc	+2	0.74
Lithium	+1	0.60	Zirconium	+4	0.80

To attain the argon configuration (*its* "nearest" noble gas), it must gain an electron to complete the $3p_z$ orbital.

An obvious solution to the electron-transfer problem would be to put sodium and chlorine atoms together to form the strongly bound compound, sodium chloride. The chemical bond so produced is called an *ionic bond*. Actually all that is required to form sodium chloride is to combine sodium and chloride ions; they need not actually exchange the same electrons. As the result of the gain or loss of an electron there is a change in the size of the ions (Fig. 3-4). The sodium ion (radius = 0.95Å) is smaller than the sodium atom (radius = 1.91Å) because the nuclear charge now pulls on only ten electrons instead of the original 11, causing a contraction. Similarly, the additional electron in the chloride ion causes it to expand (chlorine atom "covalent" radius = 0.99Å, chloride ion radius = 1.81Å).

Packing of Ions into Crystals

The ionic bond is not directional the way the covalent bond is. Hence, oppositely charged ions in a crystal stack together as compactly as possible while balancing charges on a short-range basis. For example, layers or clusters of ions of like charge are not permitted because the repulsive forces within each layer or cluster would make the assemblage unstable. In the electrically *stable* assemblage, each positive ion is surrounded with the largest number of negative ions, and vice versa (see Fig. 3-5). Relative sizes of the cation and the anion actually determine the best geometry of packing. In the case of sodium chloride, each chloride is surrounded by six sodium ions and each sodium ion is surrounded by six chloride ions, thus optimizing the distribution of charges while allowing the smaller spheres to be accommodated among the larger spheres.

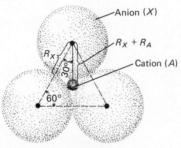

$$R_X = (R_A + R_X) \cos 30°$$

$$\frac{R_A}{R_X} = 0.145$$

Figure 3-6 Calculation of the ideal ratio of cation radius to anion radius for threefold coordination.

We can begin investigating the ideal geometries of packing by first constructing an array of anions (which are generally larger than cations, Table 3-1) that just touch each other. Holes left among the anion spheres can then accommodate a cation of the proper size; that is, the cations must be equal in size to the hole or slightly *smaller* in order to fit.

Consider first a simple case of three anions. When the spheres just touch, lines connecting their centers form an equilateral triangle (Fig. 3-6). If the radius of each anion is R_X, then the length of each side of the triangle is $2R_X$. The distance from a corner to the center of the triangle is $R_X + R_A$, where R_A is the radius of a "perfectly" fitting cation. We can calculate the ratio of cation radius to anion radius in the following manner:

$$R_X = (R_A + R_X) \cos 30°$$

since half the angle of an equilateral triangle is 30° and

$$R_X (1 - \cos 30°) = R_A$$
$$\frac{R_A}{R_X} = 1 - \cos 30° = 0.145$$

This means that the radius of the ideally sized cation must be 0.145 times the radius of the anion.

We can make similar geometric calculations for a square (planar array of four anions), a tetrahedron (three-dimensional array of four anions), an octahedron (six anions at the corner of an octahedron), and a cube (eight anions at the corners of a cube). These configurations are shown in Fig. 3-7.

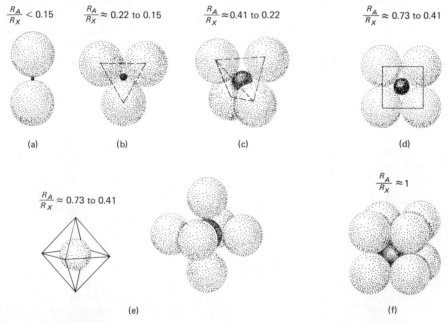

$\frac{R_A}{R_X} < 0.15$ $\qquad$ $\frac{R_A}{R_X} \approx 0.22$ to 0.15 $\qquad$ $\frac{R_A}{R_X} \approx 0.41$ to 0.22 $\qquad$ $\frac{R_A}{R_X} \approx 0.73$ to 0.41

(a) $\qquad$ (b) $\qquad$ (c) $\qquad$ (d)

$\frac{R_A}{R_X} \approx 0.73$ to 0.41 $\qquad\qquad\qquad$ $\frac{R_A}{R_X} \approx 1$

(e) $\qquad$ (f)

Figure 3-7 Ideal geometric configuration of packing for different anion-to-cation ratios.

The number of ions that any given ion touches is called its *coordination number*. Hence the triangle formed by anions provides a *threefold coordination* about a cation contained in the interior; a square and a tetrahedron each provide *fourfold coordination;* an octahedron, *sixfold coordination;* and a cube, *eightfold coordination.*

(It is important to note that for charge stabilization, if singly charged cations and anions only are involved, they both must have the same coordination number. If the cation is doubly charged and the anion singly charged, each anion will have half the coordination number of the cation. The reverse is true if the anion is doubly charged and the cation is singly charged.)

Table 3-2 summarizes all the geometric results we shall be using.

Table 3-2 Coordination Polyhedra in Ionic Bonding

Radius Ratio (R_A/R_X)	Maximum Number of Large Anions (X) Around Small Cations (A)	Coordination of X Around A
~1.00	12	as for CCP or HCP
1.00–0.73	8	at corners of a cube
0.73–0.41	{ 6	at corners of an octahedron
	{ 4	at corners of a square
0.41–0.22	4	at corners of a tetrahedron
0.22–0.15	3	at corners of a triangle
<0.15	2	linear, on opposite sides of A

THE METALLIC BOND

The packing together of atoms of a metal is constrained only by the relative sizes of the atoms. The pure metallic bond depends neither on an ionic type of electron transfer nor upon a strong directional covalency. The bonding is caused by the fact that the electrons are free to move about in the metal and this mobility provides the mechanism of supply and removal of electrons on a time-averaged basis in all the orbitals, thus satisfying the electronic condition for bonding discussed above.

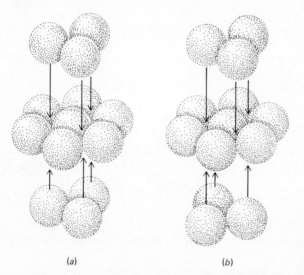

(a)   (b)

Figure 3-8 Stacking of spheres in (a) cubic closest packing and (b) hexagonal closest packing. Both have 12-fold coordination.

For example, equal-sized spheres can be arranged into *hexagonal closest packing* (HCP) or *cubic closest packing* (CCP) (Fig. 3-8). In both cases each sphere is surrounded by 12 "nearest neighbors." In hexagonal closest packing, alternate layers have the same relationship to each other as is evident in Fig. 3-8. In cubic closest packing, each atom is surrounded by 12 other atoms all equally distant from the central atom. This arrangement can be visualized by constructing a cube and putting

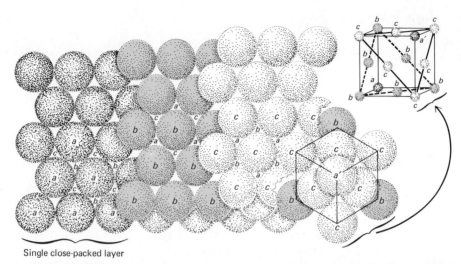

Single close-packed layer

Figure 3-9 Cubic closest packing can be regarded as a "face-centered cube" with a maximal number of "slip planes" — that is, planes along which displacement can take place without disturbing the basic packing structure. (After F. D. Bloss, see References).

atoms on each corner and at the center of each face of the cube (Fig. 3-9). If we have two such cubes sharing one face, the atom in the shared face is equidistant from 12 atoms on the two adjoining cubes. For this reason, cubic closest packing is also described as *face-centered cubic packing* (f.c.c.). This property of cubic closest packing provides the maximal number of *slip planes,* along which distortion can take place (Fig. 3-9). For this reason, elements such as silver, copper, and gold, which are stacked in cubic closest packing, are extremely ductile and malleable. Hexagonal closest packing has only one slip plane, hence metals having this form of packing are generally more brittle and less malleable than those with cubic closest packing.

Some pure metals and many alloys in particular do not observe the closest packed relationship. A very common packing pattern is one in which an atom is found on each corner of an imaginary cube in which an additional atom is placed in the center or the "body" of the cube. This packing is called *body-centered cubic packing* (b.c.c.) (Fig. 3-10).

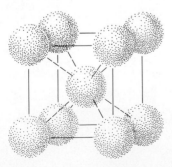

Figure 3-10 Body-centered cubic packing in metals and alloys is an eightfold coordination packing, hence not a closest packed structure

OTHER TYPES OF BONDS

Weaker bonds such as those involving the hydrogen atom exist in water and in compounds making up some rocks in the earth. These have been called *hydrogen bonds*. Even weaker bonds exist—for instance, between atoms of noble gases that have been condensed as liquids or crystals at very low temperatures. These latter very weak bonds have been described as the result of residual or *van der Waals forces*.

References

BLOSS, F.D., *Crystallography and Crystal Chemistry*. New York: Holt, Rinehart and Winston, Inc., 1971, 545 pp.

PAULING, L.C., *The Nature of the Chemical Bond and the Structure of Molecules and Crystals; an Introduction to Modern Structural Chemistry*. Ithaca, N.Y. Cornell Univ. Press, 1960, 644 pp. (3rd ed.).

4 Minerals

The solid state of matter is overwhelmingly represented by what we referred to in Chapter 3 as *crystals,* that is, ordered arrays of atoms chemically bonded together. This ordered array of bonded atoms makes a repeating pattern, which is commonly called a *lattice.* Naturally occurring solids in the crystalline state are called *minerals.*

Minerals are easily divided into two major groups: the *silicates* and the *nonsilicates.* Aside from the presumed iron-nickel core of the earth, our planet is composed primarily of silicate minerals. That is, the mineral structures and compositions are dominated by the stacking of bonded silicon and oxygen atoms in different ways.

The nonsilicates include an extremely diverse assortment of compounds that range from iron-nickel alloys to salt — their only similarity being that their structures and compositions do not depend on the silicon-oxygen bond.

We shall first discuss the silicates and then return to the nonsilicates at the end of the chapter.

SILICATES

The Silicon-Oxygen Tetrahedron

From the discussion in Chapter 3 we note that four oxygen ions have the possibility of packing together either as a square or a tetrahedron. Of the two, the tetrahedron represents the closest packing (Table 3-2). The hole left by the tetrahedrally stacked oxygen spheres (ionic radius = 1.40 Å) can just perfectly accommodate the silicon ion (ionic radius = 0.41 Å). The resulting tetrahedral coordination is further strengthened by the fact that silicon-oxygen bonds are at least partially covalent. The silicon atom has two $3s$ and two $3p$ electrons which can form four hybrid $3sp^3$ bonds pointing to the corners of a tetrahedron (Fig. 4-1), much like the $2sp^3$ bonds of carbon in the diamond structure discussed in Chapter 3. The oxygen atoms then combine with the silicon atom by sharing electron orbitals at the corners of the tetrahedron.

The net result of the combination of one Si^{+4} and four O^{-2} (in the case of the ionic bonding model) or SiO_4^{-4} (for the covalent bonding model) is a unit called the *silicon-*

oxygen tetrahedron. The silicon-oxygen tetrahedron is the fundamental unit of the normal rock-forming minerals.

Individual Silicon-Oxygen Tetrahedron

The minus four (-4) charge on an individual silicon-oxygen tetrahedron is neutralized in aqueous solutions (such as stream water and seawater) by four positively charged hydrogen ions (Fig. 4-1).

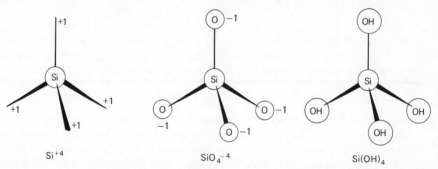

Figure 4-1 The sp^3 hybridized orbitals of silicon with the addition of oxygen atoms at each tetrahedral arm and then hydrogen.

In solids, the charge on the tetrahedron can be accommodated by a variety of other methods. The simplest is to bind silicon-oxygen tetrahedra together with cations. Such a configuration is found in the mineral *olivine* (Fig. 4-2), whose chemical formula can be written: (two octahedral doubly charged cations) + (one quadruply charged silicon cation) + (four doubly charged oxygen anions), with a net charge of zero.

The common cations that participate in the olivine structure are iron and magnesium. The ionic radii of Fe^{+2} and Mg^{+2}, 0.76 and 0.65 Å, respectively, are ideal for

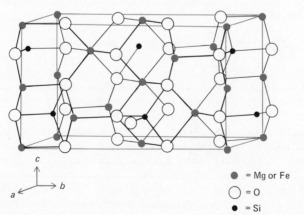

c

a *b*

● = Mg or Fe

○ = O

● = Si

Figure 4-2 The atomic structure of olivine.

the octahedrally coordinated site. The chemical formula of olivine then can be written:

$$Fe_2SiO_4 \quad \text{or} \quad Mg_2SiO_4$$

It turns out that in nature the Fe^{+2} and Mg^{+2} can substitute freely for each other, and most olivines are mixtures of the pure *end members*. Names are given to the pure end members: Fe_2SiO_4 is called *fayalite* and Mg_2SiO_4 is called *forsterite*. It is a common practice then to write the general formula as $(Fe, Mg)_2SiO_4$.

Different proportions of Mg^{+2} and Fe^{+2} may be expressed quantitatively as *solid solutions* of the two end members. If we denote 100 percent Fe_2SiO_4 (fayalite) as Fa_{100}, then a mixture of the two end members in which, say, the number of atoms of Fe^{+2} and Mg^{+2} are equal is written Fa_{50}. A ratio of $4Fe^{+2}$ to $1Mg^{+2}$ is written Fa_{80} (since 80 percent of the olivine can be thought of as being fayalite) and so forth.

Other common minerals involving the stacking of individual silicon-oxygen tetrahedra with cations are the garnets and zircon $(ZrSiO_4)$. The garnet family of minerals is particularly complex, allowing a wide range of substitutions and co-ordinations as seen in Table 4-1.

Table 4-1 Composition of Some Ideal Garnets[a]

Name	Formula	Coordinations		
		4	6	8
pyrope	$Mg_3Al_2(SiO_4)_3$	Si^{+4}	Al^{+3}	Mg^{+2}
almandine	$Fe_3Al_2(SiO_4)_3$	Si^{+4}	Al^{+3}	Fe^{+2}
spessartite	$Mn_3Al_2(SiO_4)_3$	Si^{+4}	Al^{+3}	Mn^{+2}
grossularite	$Ca_3Al_2(SiO_4)_3$	Si^{+4}	Al^{+3}	Ca^{+2}
andradite	$Ca_3Fe_2(SiO_4)_3$	Si^{+4}	Fe^{+3}	Ca^{+2}
uvarovite	$Ca_3Cr_2(SiO_4)_3$	Si^{+4}	Cr^{+3}	Ca^{+2}

[a]Actually, most garnets are "mixtures" of these ideal types.

Polymerization of Silicon-Oxygen Tetrahedra

Aside from the cation "glue," which serves to neutralize the negative charge of the silicon-oxygen tetrahedra, it is also possible to relieve the charge requirements by varying degrees of *polymerization,* or linking together of the tetrahedra themselves. For instance, one of the tetrahedral oxygens can be shared by two silicon atoms to give the unit $Si_2O_7^{-6}$ (Fig. 4-3). Although a few minerals with this unit have been found, the common minerals have a higher degree of polymerization.

One possibility is a ring made by joining six tetrahedra together so that two of the four oxygens linked to each silicon are shared with neighboring silicon atoms (Fig. 4-3). The mineral *beryl* is made of such rings stacked vertically in columns (Fig. 4-4). (The gem form of beryl is called *emerald*.) The corridors made within such hollow columns provide traps for atoms, in particular the chemically inert noble gases such as argon and helium. Such trapping structures are called *clathrate* (or "cage") structures.

The other types of polymerization of silicon-oxygen tetrahedra include the *chain,* the *double chain,* the *sheet,* and the *framework* (Fig. 4-3). We can now discuss the remainder of the major rock-forming silicate minerals in the context of these different structures.

(a) Isolated tetrahedra: $\left[SiO_4\right]^{-4}$

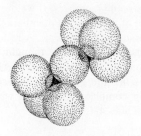

(b) Double tetrahedra: $\left[Si_2O_7\right]^{-6}$

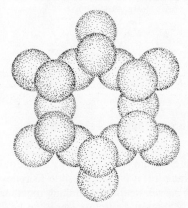

(c) Six-sided ring $\left[SiO_3\right]^{-2}$

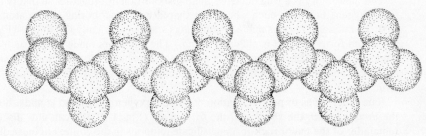

(d) Single chain: $\left[SiO_3\right]^{-2}$

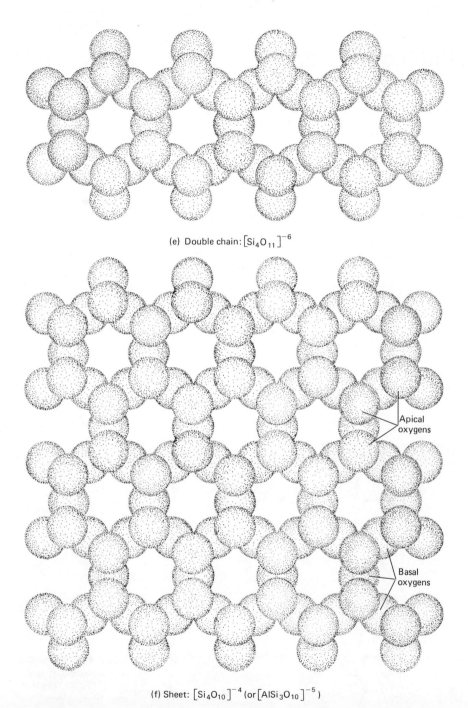

(e) Double chain: $\left[Si_4O_{11}\right]^{-6}$

(f) Sheet: $\left[Si_4O_{10}\right]^{-4}$ (or $\left[AlSi_3O_{10}\right]^{-5}$)

Figure 4-3 The polymerization of silicon oxygen tetrahedra. In addition to the configurations shown there is the ultimate polymerization in a three-dimensional framework configuration.

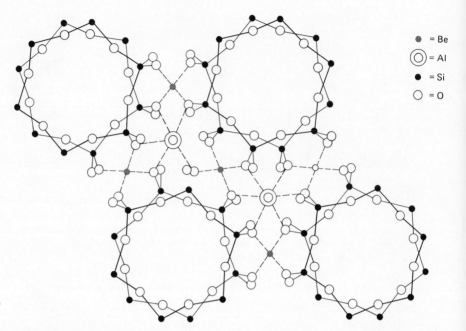

Figure 4-4 The atomic structure of beryl ($Be_3Al_2Si_6O_{18}$), looking down an axis perpendicular to the ring structure.

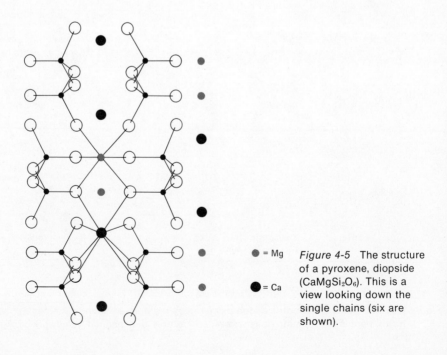

Figure 4-5 The structure of a pyroxene, diopside ($CaMgSi_2O_6$). This is a view looking down the single chains (six are shown).

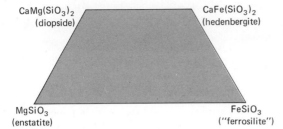

CaMg(SiO₃)₂
(diopside)

CaFe(SiO₃)₂
(hedenbergite)

MgSiO₃
(enstatite)

FeSiO₃
("ferrosilite")

Figure 4-6 The composition range of pyroxenes. Most pyroxenes are either calcium-rich or calcium-poor with very few examples in the middle of the field.

Pyroxenes

In *pyroxene* the *single chain* polymers of silicon-oxygen tetrahedra are held together by cations (Fig. 4-5). The cations are commonly in octahedral coordination and are thus primarily restricted to Fe^{+2} and Mg^{+2}, as in the case of olivines. However, Ca^{+2} may substitute in some of the larger sites in eightfold coordination. The range of compositions in naturally occurring pyroxenes is commonly shown in a triangular composition diagram, in which iron, magnesium, and calcium pyroxenes are the corners of the triangle. Solid solutions of these three end members are limited to the field shown in Fig. 4-6.

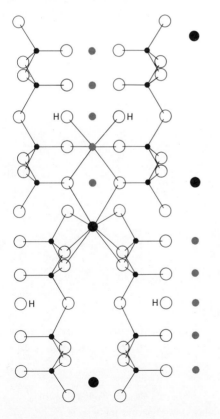

H   H

H

H   H

● = Mg

● = Ca

Figure 4-7 The structure of an amphibole, actinolite $(Mg_5Ca_2Si_8O_{22}(OH)_2)$. This is a view looking down the double chains (four are shown).

Pyroxenes are one of the two fundamental minerals in basalts—the common rocks of oceanic islands as well as in many places on the continents. Pyroxene is also common in stone meteorites and the moon.

Amphiboles

Double chains of silicon-oxygen tetrahedra held together commonly by the cations Mg^{+2}, Fe^{+2}, and Ca^{+2} (with some of the oxygens attached to hydrogen ions) are called *amphiboles* (Fig. 4-7). The range of chemical composition in amphiboles is much

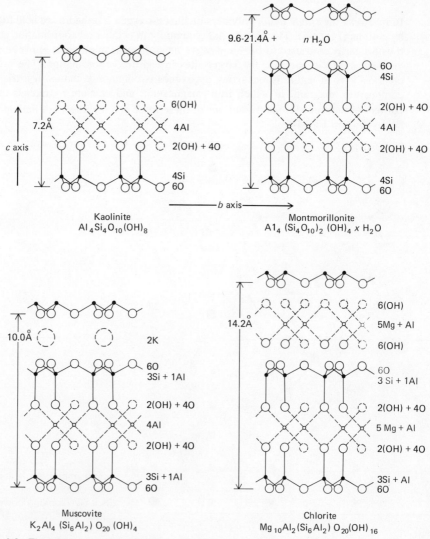

Figure 4-8   The structures of the layered silicates viewed across the sheets.

greater than in pyroxenes (for example, the amphibole series called *hornblende* has the general equation $Ca_2Na_{0-1}(Mg,Fe,Al)_5[(Al,Si)_4O_{11}]_2(OH)_2$). Amphiboles are found predominantly in continental rocks, but they are not entirely restricted to the continents. Some occurrences along fracture zones in the deep ocean have been reported.

Micas and Clay Minerals

Silicon-oxygen tetrahedra that are polymerized into *infinite sheets* form layered minerals such as the micas and clay minerals. In *muscovite* (Fig. 4-8), one quarter of the tetrahedrally bound silicon ions (charge $= +4$, ionic radius $= 0.41$Å) are replaced by aluminum ions (charge $= +3$, ionic radius $= 0.50$Å). The additional positive charge that is "lost" by this exchange is provided by a large potassium ion (charge $= +1$, ionic radius $= 1.33$ Å) inserted between the layers. Each sheet is a three-part Si^{+4}, one-part Al^{+3} tetrahedral layer bound through octahedrally coordinated Al^{+3} to another tetrahedral sheet. This tetrahedral-octahedral-tetrahedral sheet is tied to adjacent sheets through the large intersheet potassium ions.

The dominance of Mg^{+2} and Fe^{+2} in the octahedral sites results in the black mica, or *biotite*.

The *clay minerals* are produced by the weathering of rocks or by the action of hot water or hot water vapor on other silicate minerals. Most clay minerals are very fine grained. Their structures, however, are basically the layered lattice structures seen in the micas, with some significant differences caused by modifications of the basic structure through rearrangements and chemical substitutions (Fig. 4-8).

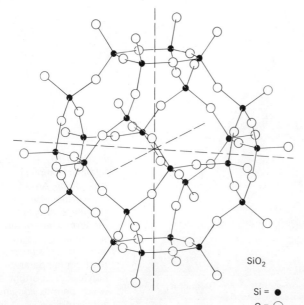

SiO_2

$Si = \bullet$
$O = \bigcirc$

Figure 4-9   The structure of quartz.

Quartz

Common especially in continental rocks, *quartz* has a *framework* structure of silicon-oxygen tetrahedra. In the framework structure all the oxygen atoms of the silicon-oxygen tetrahedra are each shared by two silicon atoms. The structure results in a ratio of one silicon to two oxygen atoms, hence there is no need for additional cations to attain neurtality (Fig. 4-9).

The tetrahedra in a framework SiO_2 structure can be connected in a number of different ways to produce different *polymorphs* in the same way that graphite and diamond are polymorphs of carbon. For example, *coesite* is a polymorph of SiO_2 that is stable at very high pressures. Its presence in meteorite craters is compatible with the high pressures generated there by the impacting meteorite.

Feldspars

The ionic radius of the aluminum ion is just right to permit it to enter either into six-fold or fourfold coordination. In the example of the layered silicates given above we have already seen that this multiple coordination is common. In the framework silicates, Al^{+3} can substitute for Si^{+4} in tetrahedral coordination. The large "holes" in the open framework structure then allow the extra positive charge required for each Al^{+3}–Si^{+4} substitution to be filled by the common alkali metals such as sodium and potassium and the common alkaline-earth metal, calcium.

In the structure of a *feldspar* exactly one aluminum replaces one silicon out of four. That is, if we start with four Si^{+4} + eight O^{-2} (which would be a quartz composition) and replace one of the four Si^{+4} with one Al^{+3} + one K^{+1} (or Na^{+1}), the charge is balanced and we get the chemical compositions $KAlSi_3O_8$ (*orthoclase*) or $NaAlSi_3O_8$ (*albite*). A limited solid solution series exists between these two end members but the large difference in ionic radii prohibits it from being complete.

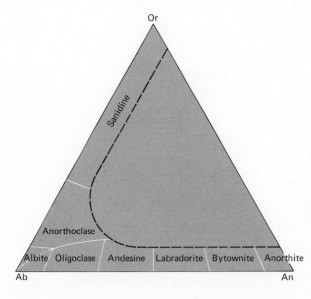

Figure 4-10   The range of feldspar compositions. Ab = albite, An = anorthite, Or = orthoclase, as end members. *Anorthoclase* is the term used for albite with some potassium substitution; *sanidine* is the high temperature polymorph of orthoclase which permits sodium substitution.

The similar radii of the sodium and calcium ions ($Na^{+1} = 0.95$; $Ca^{+2} = 0.99$) should make mutual substitution easy. There is one complication, however. For every substitution of a Ca^{+2} for an Na^{+1} in a feldspar lattice an additional substitution of a tetrahedral Al^{+3} for Si^{+4} must take place. This can proceed until all the sodiums have been substituted by calcium ions. The calcium feldspar is called *anorthite:* $CaAlSi_2O_8$.

The NaSi for CaAl substitution, when formed at high temperature, is called the *plagioclase* solid solution series to distinguish it from the potassium feldspar and its limited solid solution series with sodium feldspar. The range of feldspar composition is shown in Fig. 4-10.

Other Framework Silicates

The next jump in substitution in the SiO_2 framework structure is to substitute two Al^{+3} for two Si^{+4} with the charge deficiency made up by further addition of sodium or potassium. The minerals so constructed are called *feldspathoids* (or minerals resembling feldspars). They are *nepheline* ($NaAlSiO_4$) and *kaliophillite* ($KAlSiO_4$). Another option is the replacement of one third of the Si^{+4} with the $K^{+1} + Al^{+3}$ combination, resulting in the mineral *leucite* ($KAlSi_2O_6$).

The last group of framework silicates we shall consider have structures based on the substitution of one third of the Si^{+4} by Al^{+3}, resulting in a more open structure than that possessed by either the feldspars or the feldspathoids. This class of complexly substituted framework silicates is called the *zeolites*. A typical composition is *analcime* ($NaAlSi_2O_6 \cdot H_2O$). The holes in this framework structure are occupied (in a definite fashion) by both Na^{+1} and H_2O.

Zeolites, both natural and artificially made, can have a property resembling the action of a "sieve" on a molecular level. "Smooth" organic molecules slip through the molecular sieve made by the zeolite lattice whereas "jagged" organic molecules get caught. The usefulness of this property for chemical separation and purification is obvious.

NONSILICATE MINERALS

A number of important minerals are not based upon the silicate structure. Rather than review the whole range of common nonsilicate minerals (some of whose compositions are given in Table 4-2), we shall explore a few selected compounds. We

Table 4-2 Composition of Some Common Nonsilicate Minerals

Mineral Name	Chemical Composition	Mineral Name	Chemical Composition
graphite	C	hematite	Fe_2O_3
diamond	C	chalcopyrite	$CuFeS_2$
halite	NaCl	sphalerite	ZnS
calcite	$CaCO_3$	gypsum	$CaSO_4 \cdot 2H_2O$
aragonite	$CaCO_3$	anhydrite	$CaSO_4$
pyrite	FeS_2	fluorite	CaF_2
galena	PbS	apatite	$Ca_5(PO_4)_3(OH,F,Cl)$
magnetite	Fe_3O_4	cassiterite	SnO_2

have already discussed graphite, diamond, sodium chloride (the mineral *halite*) and the metals in order to illustrate chemical bonding. In addition we shall look at *fluorite* (CaF_2), *calcite* ($CaCO_3$), and *pyrite* (FeS_2).

Fluorite

With the ionic radii of calcium and fluoride being 0.99 Å and 1.36 Å, respectively, a radius ratio of Ca^{+2} to F^{-1} equal to 0.73 results, which is just right for the eightfold (or cubic) coordination (Table 3-2) of calcium by eight fluorine ions (Fig. 4-11). But since there must be twice as many fluoride ions as calcium ions for charge satisfaction, each fluoride ion is surrounded by only four calcium ions.

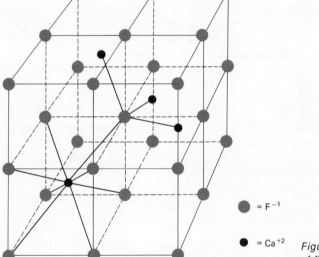

● = F^{-1}

● = Ca^{+2} *Figure 4-11*   The structure of fluorite.

Calcite

As indicated in Chapter 3, carbon in the carbonate radical is covalently bonded with three oxygens. The resulting unit has great stability in the form of a compact equilateral triangle of oxygens. The carbonate (CO_3^{-2}) ion behaves then as an irregularly shaped unit and enters into simple ionic bonding. When stacked with Ca^{+2}, an octahedral coordination for both the Ca^{-2} and CO_3^{-2} results, just as in the sodium chloride structure. A big difference, however, is that the carbonate ion is not a sphere but a triangle. In closest packing, the triangles are oriented in the same plane resulting in a distortion of the simple lattice expected from the sodium chloride analog (Fig. 4-12).

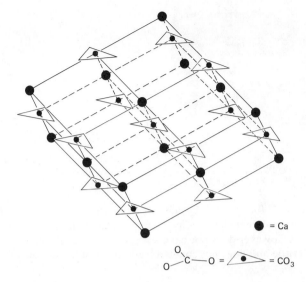

● = Ca

$_O^O{>}C-O = \triangleright$ • $\triangleright$ = CO_3

Figure 4-12 The structure of calcite.

Pyrite

In pyrite, two sulfur atoms are covalently joined together into dumbbells, which in turn are bonded ionically with Fe^{+2} in octahedral coordination (Fig. 4-13). The distortion in the atomic structure of the crystal due to the nonspherical S-S dumbbells is manifested as striations (grooves) on the surface of pyrite crystals (Fig. 4-14).

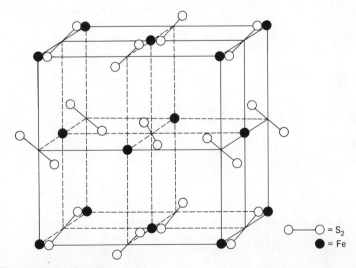

○—○ = S_2
● = Fe

Figure 4-13   The structure of pyrite.

Figure 4-14 The surface manifestation of the covalent *S-S* dumbbells seen as striations on crystal surfaces.

Pyrite is also known as "fool's gold" because of its bright, goldlike luster. This indicates that there is a small metallic bonding component in addition to the ionic-covalent bonding. Pyrite however does not have some of the most distinctive properties of metals. It is brittle and does not conduct a current well the way metals do.

References

BERRY, L. G., and B. MASON, *Mineralogy: Concepts, Descriptions, Determinations.* San Francisco, Calif.: W. H. Freeman and Co., 1959, 612 pp.

BLOSS, F. D., *Crystallography and Crystal Chemistry.* New York: Holt, Rinehart and Winston, 1971, 545 pp.

FYFE, W. S., *Geochemistry of Solids: An Introduction.* New York: McGraw-Hill Book Co., 1964, 199 pp.

5 Rocks

Rocks — assemblages of mineral grains — are the most common material of the earth. For this reason, most of us take them for granted and ignore their existence in all but the most compelling circumstances. It is obvious to everyone that mountains are made of rock, but it is not always evident that the vast plains of all the continents are made of the same material as these jagged mountains.

There are many different kinds of rocks, having different chemical and mineralogical compositions, hardnesses, and other properties. It is the study of these qualities of rocks and the processes responsible for them that is the concern of the *petrologist*.

The most elementary classification of rocks is based on the mode of formation. Three major groups are recognized: igneous, sedimentary, and metamorphic. *Igneous* rocks appear to have been formed from the molten state. Rocks that are the indurated (hardened) deposits of materials carried and deposited by wind, streams, or oceanic action are called *sedimentary* rocks. With heating, application of pressure, and with some chemical change, rocks of igneous or sedimentary origin may be transformed into *metamorphic* rocks.

In this chapter we shall explore the varieties of rock and their modes of origin. Many igneous and metamorphic rocks are formed at high enough temperatures that reactions can rapidly approach chemical equilibrium. That is, the individual coexisting mineral grains can be shown from laboratory studies to have been formed at a common temperature. (For a discussion of the concept of chemical equilibrium see the Appendix.) Chemical equilibrium is less likely for sedimentary rocks, whose mineral associations mainly reflect the debris of rocks destroyed by biological activity and the manner of transport and deposition from flowing air and water.

IGNEOUS ROCKS

We indicated above that igneous rocks crystallized from molten material. The molten material is called *magma*. Where a magma is seen on the surface of the earth it is called *lava*, and the rock that solidifies from it is called an *extrusive* rock. It is evi-

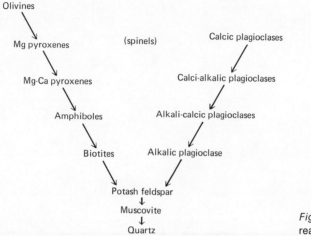

Olivines

Mg pyroxenes   (spinels)   Calcic plagioclases

Mg-Ca pyroxenes   Calci-alkalic plagioclases

Amphiboles   Alkali-calcic plagioclases

Biotites   Alkalic plagioclase

Potash feldspar
↓
Muscovite
↓
Quartz

Figure 5-1   Bowen's
reaction series.

dent that the magma may also crystallize at great depth in a large chamber or in the midst of rocks in which it has halted during its rise towards the surface. Igneous rocks formed upon the solidification of this magma are called *intrusive* rocks.

In addition, we may classify igneous rocks on the basis of mineralogical composition, which in turn reflects the composition of the magma and the temperature of formation of the rock.

A useful generalization can be obtained by a plot of the sequence of minerals that would be formed if a magma were allowed to cool gradually (Fig. 5-1). This so-called *reaction series* was conceived by N. L. Bowen, who was also one of the first sucessful experimentalists in the field of petrology.

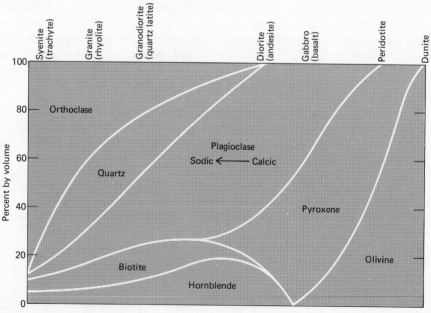

Figure 5-2   Range of common rock types and their mineralogies. Parentheses indicate name of equivalent extrusive rock.

Figure 5–3 The Hawaiian islands—Kilauea Crater. Courtesy of the Hawaii Visitors Bureau.

Figure 5-4 The lava flows of the Pacific Northwest. From *The Earth: An Introduction to Physical Geology* by John Verhoogen, Francis J. Turner, Lionel E. Weiss, Clyde Wahrhaftig, and William S. Fyfe. Copyright © 1970 by Holt, Rinehart and Winston, Inc. Reproduced by permission of Holt, Rinehart and Winston, Inc.

Basalt is typically made up of olivine, pyroxene, and calcium-rich plagioclase. An assemblage of sodium-rich plagioclase, potassium feldspar (orthoclase and other polymorphs), and quartz is typical of *granitic rocks*. These two types (with variants) make up the largest quantity of igneous rock.

Figure 5-2 shows the range of rock types and the proportions of the different common minerals.

Basaltic Rocks

The principal igneous rocks of the oceanic domain are of basaltic affinities. The Hawaiian Islands (Fig. 5-3), the Azores, and hundreds of other volcanic islands in the oceans are composed of variants of the basaltic composition. Samples returned from dredging of the ocean floor make it evident that most of the ocean floor is underlain by basaltic rocks.

Basaltic rocks are found also on the continents, where they are commonly seen as gigantic outpourings of lava that form large plateaus. One of the most spectacular piles is seen in the U.S. Pacific Northwest, where the Snake and Columbia Rivers have cut through layer upon layer of lava flows (Fig. 5-4).

On the continents they can also occur as rather shallow intrusive rocks. A rising magma can follow a variety of paths according to where it can most easily be accommodated. If it oozes up along preexisting cracks, created by tension in the rocks, the resulting intrusive rock is called a *dike*. In fact, all magma reaching the surface must have flowed through such cracks. A dike may be commonly found as a supplier or "feeder" for other intrusive rocks as well as for extrusive rocks (Fig. 5-5).

If magma is injected along previously deposited layers of sediments or volcanic rocks, for example, the intrusion is called a *sill* (Fig. 5-5). The Palisades of New Jersey, across from the city of New York, is an example of a sill. An even more famous example is the Great Whin Sill in Northumberland, England, along which the Romans built a wall to protect conquered England from the unconquered Celtic

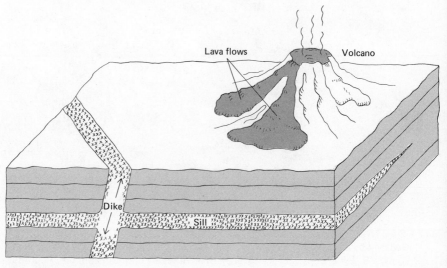

Figure 5-5 Dikes and sills.

tribes in the North. Because most dikes and sills are emplaced at relatively shallow depths in the earth's crust, they are called *hypabyssal* intrusives.

Less abundant are the deeply emplaced *abyssal* basaltic rocks. They are important in the study of the modes of origin and emplacement of basaltic rocks because they represent vats of magma undergoing slow cooling and crystal formation. The minerals forming at any particular temperature are always denser than the melt. They settle through the magma under the force of gravity and accumulate in stratified deposits, recording sequentially upward the changing composition of the magma as it crystallized.

There are several well-studied bodies (or "complexes"): the Skaergaard Complex in Greenland, the Bushveld Complex in South Africa, the Stillwater Complex in Montana, and the Musk Ox Complex in Canada. Although no two of these are identical, they *do* all show how magmas can be altered in large magma chambers and how the alteration may lead to a variety of basaltic rocks. Figure 5-6 is a cross section of the Stillwater Complex, showing how each layer varies in composition. The pattern roughly follows that expected from experimentally determined phase diagrams (see Appendix).

The primary source of basaltic magma is the *upper mantle* of the earth—that is, the layer just below the outermost layer, called the *crust*. A variety of lines of evidence, listed in the next chapter, indicate that the upper mantle is composed of a more magnesium- and iron-rich and sodium- and potassium-poor rock than basalt. Thus we have the problem of extracting a basaltic liquid from upper mantle rocks of a more magnesium- and iron-rich nature. A study of Hawaiian volcanism and associated earthquake activity indicates that basalt is generated in large quantities at a depth of about 50 kilometers beneath the ocean bottom.

Not all the variations in basalt can be explained by partial crystallization of a single parent magma. For this reason we believe that there is some degree of inhomogeneity in the upper mantle, resulting in slight nuances in the composition of basalt reaching the surface. Variations in pressure, and reaction of the magma with the surrounding rock during slow ascent, may also create strong differences among basalt magmas by the time they reach the surface. We have already made considerable progress in unraveling these effects using laboratory experiments in conjunction with the observations out in the field.

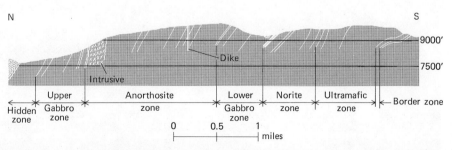

Figure 5-6 Mineral layering in the Stillwater Complex of Montana. The bottom of the chamber in which the magma crystallized is to the south. The sequence upward resembles Bowen's reaction series (Fig. 5-1). Ultramafic rocks include peridotite; the norite, gabbro and anorthosite rocks progressively have plagioclases more and more enriched in sodium and pyroxenes more and more enriched in iron. Secondary dikes intersect the complex. After H. H. Hess, Geological Society of America, Memoir 80 (1960).

Granitic Rocks

Whereas basaltic rocks underlie the ocean basins and are also found on continents, the granitic rocks are almost exclusively restricted to the continents.

The source of most granite is probably not the mantle as it is with basalts (even though fractional crystallization of a basaltic magma ideally could lead to a small amount of granitic material). It has been shown in the laboratory that if a mixture of muscovite, quartz, the clay mineral kaolinite, and sodium chloride with varying amounts of calcium carbonate are subjected to temperatures of 600°C and higher, under steam pressures equivalent to several tens of kilometers of depth in the earth's crust, a melt of granitic composition forms. The starting materials are what we can expect as normal products of weathering and sedimentation – that is, materials we might find on the seashore or on the sea bottom. Could it be that granites originate at least in part by heating of wet, salty sediments under high, confining pressures? This thought had been expressed about 150 years ago, but only recent experiments seem to confirm it. This does not rule out a true igneus origin for some rocks of granitic affinity. The case for this type of formation is seen in the granitic affinity rocks found in the oceanic island arcs such as Japan.

Granitic rocks can be both extrusive and intrusive rocks but most commonly

Figure 5-7   The Sierra Nevada batholith as seen at Yosemite Park in California. Ansel Adams.

they are the latter. Extensive granitic terranes are sometimes called *batholiths*. Some common examples in the United States are the Sierra Nevada batholith (Fig. 5-7) and the Idaho batholith. The relationship of granites to other rocks in nature is quite variable, their common quality being that they are associated with mountains — either actual mountains or the roots of ancient mountains beveled off by erosion.

In summary, the granitic composition is best characterized as the "lowest melting" fraction extractable from a melange of sedimentary and previously deposited igneous rocks. Fractional crystallization is most clearly seen in the form of *pegmatites* — small deposits with large crystals most often associated with granitic and metamorphic terranes and commonly concentrated in rare elements.

SEDIMENTARY ROCKS

After a rock has been degraded under the chemical and physical assault of living organisms and the weather, the resulting particulate and dissolved products can be transported away from the site of weathering by streams, glaciers, and wind. The transported material that is finally deposited somewhere else is called *sediment*.

Sediment may either be *detrital* (physically transported particles), *biological* (extracted from solution by organisms), or *chemical* (deposited from solution by inorganic processes).

Figure 5-8 The Grand Canyon showing cliffs of limestone and sandstone. With permission of the Union Pacific Railroad.

When the deposited sediment is subjected to moderate heat and pressure and the action of intergranular water as the result of burial, the sediment is changed to a more cohesive state and is called *sedimentary rock*. The hardnesses of sedimentary rocks are highly variable. Some sediments may remain close to their original state of disaggregation and, except for the loss of water and dissolved salts, they do not look very different from newly deposited sediments. Elsewhere, bold cliffs of limestone or sandstone testify to the fact that sediments can also become highly indurated (Fig. 5-8).

Table 5-1 shows the relationship between sediments and their equivalent sedimentary rocks. We will discuss the major chemical properties of the different types of common sedimentary deposits.

Detrital Sediments

The grain sizes of solid particles carried by streams, winds, or glaciers range from boulders to mud. Generally, the finer grained the sediment the farther it can be transported from its source by moving fluids. The boulders faithfully represent the compositions of the rocks from which they were derived. The sand size fraction, on the other hand, contains minerals resistant to the chemical action of weathering. Each mineral in a rock has its own resistance to weathering. Generally, among the common silicates, the most resistant are the framework silicates, with decreasing resistance with decreasing degree of silicate tetrahedra polymerization (olivine is the least resistant of the common silicates). The most common resistant mineral is quartz. However, it is not unusual to find deposits of sand-sized grains containing feldspars, and, in some cases, even pyroxenes and garnets.

The finest fraction contains the clay mineral products of weathering. In Fig. 4-8 the crystal structures and compositions of the various clay minerals were shown. *Illite* is the clay-sized equivalent of muscovite and is a common component of many rocks. Much of the illite found in sediments is directly derived with minimal chemical alteration from the disintegration of igneous, metamorphic or sedimentary rocks, although some may be made during the conversion of the sediment to sedimentary rock.

More intense weathering results in two other clay minerals — *chlorite* and *montmorillonite*. Both of these minerals have essentially the illite structure, but other

Table 5-1 Sediments and Their Equivalent Sedimentary Rocks

	Type of Sediment	Type of Sedimentary Rock
Detrital		
	mud	shale
	sand	sandstone
	gravel	conglomerate
Biological		
	seashells	limestone
	coral reefs	limestone
	diatoms	chert (or flint)
	radiolaria	chert (or flint)
Chemical		
	salt	evaporite
	gypsum	evaporite

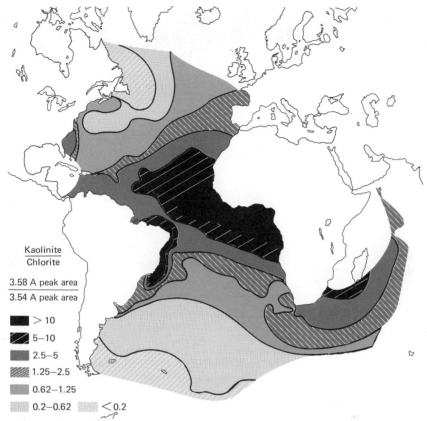

Figure 5-9 The kaolinite-chlorite ratio distribution in deep-sea sediments. Modified from P. E. Biscaye, *Bulletin of the Geological Society of America,* **76,** 803 (1965).

"cementing" chemical units instead of potassium are used to bind the aluminosilicate sheets together. In chlorite the interlayer unit is $Mg(OH)_2$, and in montmorillonite it is water and a host of exchangeable cations.

Where weathering is very intense, as in the tropics, rocks and other clay minerals already formed are further degraded to *kaolinite,* a mineral composed exclusively of aluminum octahedral and silicon tetrahedral sheets held together by hydrogen bonding. With even more intense weathering, silica leaches out, resulting in a residue of aluminum oxides and iron oxides typical of tropical *lateritic* soils.

The relative proportions of these minerals in sediments give some idea of the weathering regime on the adjacent continents. An example is the distribution of the kaolinite-to-chlorite ratio in deep-sea sediments (Fig. 5-9). Kaolinite is an index of intense weathering typical of the tropics, whereas chlorite is formed or preserved in the cooler environment of higher latitudes.

Rocks made from clay-rich sediments are called *shales*. Rocks made from sand-sized grains are called *sandstones*. Normally their mineralogy is dominated by quartz. If they are rich in feldspars they are called *arkoses,* and if they have a mixture of different kinds of mineral grains they are called *graywackes*.

(a) Pteropods (snail-like pelagic aragonitic molluscs). Size: 1 to 2 mm. Specimens Courtesy of Dr. C. Chen.

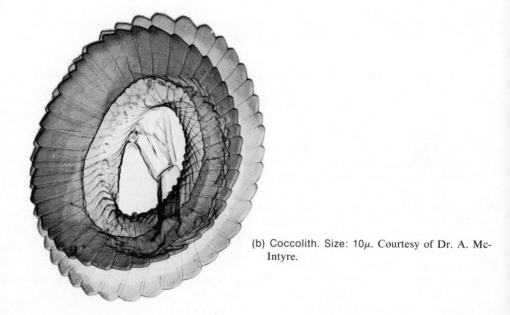

(b) Coccolith. Size: 10μ. Courtesy of Dr. A. McIntyre.

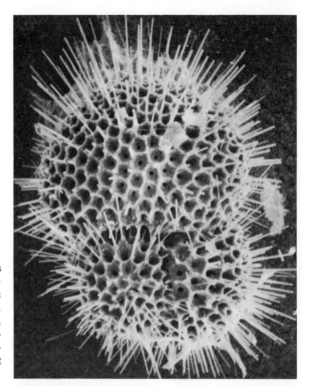

(c) Foraminifera. Globigerinoides saccrilifera (Brady) from plankton tow in tropical Atlantic Ocean. Shell length about 800μ. Courtesy of Dr. Allan W. H. Bé, *Science,* **161,** 881 (1968). Copyright 1968 by the American Association for the Advancement of Science.

(d) Clam. Quahog (Mercenaria mercenaria). Size: 5 to 10 cm. Courtesy of Dr. D. Rhoads.

(e) Coral. Brain coral. Size: 50 to 100 cm. (Kitchen for Photo Researchers).

Figure 5-10   Types of calcium-carbonate depositing organisms.

Table 5-2 Mineralogical Forms of Calcium Carbonate Deposited by Marine Organisms

	Aragonite	*Calcite*	*High-Magnesium Calcite*
Corals (scleractinian)	X		
Snails	X	X	
Clams	X	X	
Starfish			X
Foraminifera (pelagic)		X	
Coccoliths		X	

Biogenic Sediments

Marine organisms may secrete calcium carbonate ($CaCO_3$) or Silica (SiO_2), which are preserved as sedimentary deposits. The shells of most clams, snails, starfish, corals, and foraminiferans (a type of single-celled organism) are composed of calcium carbonate (Fig. 5-10). There are two polymorphs of calcium carbonate — *calcite* and *aragonite* — both of which are used by organisms in constructing skeletons. Calcite in turn is found in two distinct chemical forms, one is low in magnesium and

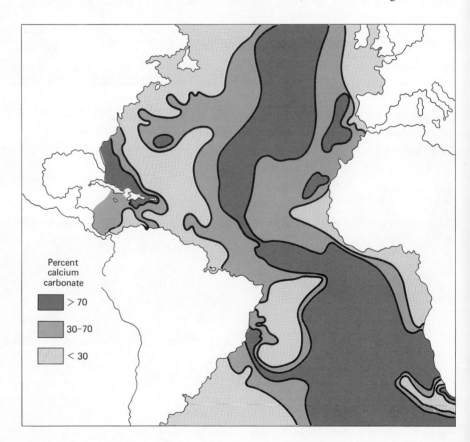

Figure 5-11 The distribution of calcium-carbonate in deep-sea sediments.

the other is high in magnesium. Table 5-2 gives the mineralogy of the major calcium carbonate depositors.

Despite the high visibility of coral reefs and clam and snail shells, these represent only a small fraction of the total calcium carbonate presently being deposited. Most of the calcium carbonate deposited in the oceans today comes from a steady "rain" of skeletons of deep-sea foraminiferans and minute single-celled floating plants (the coccolithiphorides). Figure 5-11 shows the distribution of calcium carbonate in the deep-sea sediments of the Atlantic Ocean.

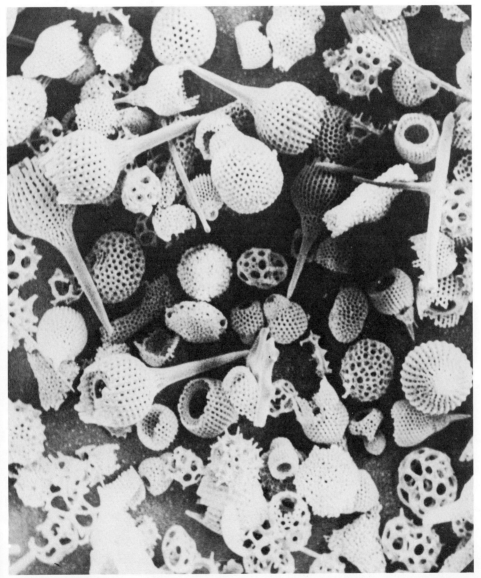

Figure 5-12   (a) Radiolaria skeletons from a core in the Western Pacific obtained by the Deep Sea Drilling Project, funded by the National Science Foundation. Size: about 100μ. Courtesy of Scripps Institution of Oceanography.

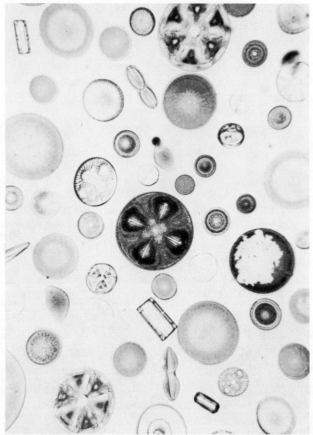

Figure 5-12   (b) Marine diatoms. Size about 500μ. Courtesy of Dr. Richard L. Smith.

Another carbonate mineral, *dolomite* (CaMg(CO₃)₂), is commonly found in old sedimentary rocks but rarely in modern deposits. It is not a primary deposit since no organism produces a dolomite shell. It is probably the reaction product of deposited calcium carbonate and magnesium ions carried in warm brines (formed by evaporation and heating in shallow basins formed in subtropical regions) in contact with it. Other mechanisms of dolomite formation are also possible, but the one mentioned is the only one that seems to be observable in the field now. Rocks formed from calcium carbonate sediments are called *limestones*.

Of the siliceous shells found in sediments, those deposited by *diatoms* and *radiolaria* are the most important (Fig. 5-12). Because these shells are so easily dissolved in seawater, they accumulate as sediments where there is both high biological productivity and high silica concentration in the water. These conditions are met in the deep sea at high latitudes—in particular, around Antarctica, along the east equatorial Pacific, and the Gulf of California, where strong nutrient and silica-rich upwelling currents are present. The major areas of silica deposition appear, however, to be near-shore bays and estuaries, but masking by abundant detrital sediments derived from the continents diminishes their visibility.

The deposited form of silica is a highly disordered, hydrated (water-containing) variety. With time, this is converted to a microcrystalline form of quartz called *chert* or *flint*. The hardness of this material made it highly desirable to the paleolithic and neolithic peoples of Europe who made tools and weapons of it.

Chemical Sediments

It has been determined that surface seawater is supersaturated with respect to calcium carbonate. Hence a precipitate of calcite or aragonite presumably could form directly from seawater. Although this process may be taking place in warm, shallow seas, like the Bahamas Platform, on a worldwide scale it is primarily biological deposition of shells that is responsible for calcium carbonate sediments.

All other chemical (that is, nonbiologically produced) deposits are the result of the isolation and solar heating of seawater in restricted basins. With continuous evaporation of seawater, the resulting brine becomes progressively saturated with respect to one chemical compound after another. Table 5-3 shows the sequence of compounds precipitated experimentally from a brine undergoing progressive evaporation.

Table 5-3 Salts Laid Down During Concentration of Seawater (grams)[a]

Volume (liters)	Fe_2O_3	$CaCO_3$	$CaSO_4$ $\cdot 2H_2O$	NaCl	$MgSO_4$	$MgCl_2$	NaBr	KCl
1.000	–	–	–	–	–	–	–	–
0.533	0.0030	0.0642	–	–	–	–	–	–
0.316	–	trace	–	–	–	–	–	–
0.245	–	trace	–	–	–	–	–	–
0.190	–	0.0530	0.5600	–	–	–	–	–
0.1445	–	–	0.5620	–	–	–	–	–
0.131	–	–	0.1840	–	–	–	–	–
0.112	–	–	0.1600	–	–	–	–	–
0.095	–	–	0.0508	3.2614	0.0040	0.0078	–	–
0.064	–	–	0.1476	9.6500	0.0130	0.0356	–	–
0.039	–	–	0.0700	7.8960	0.0262	0.0434	0.0728	–
0.0302	–	–	0.0144	2.6240	0.0174	0.0150	0.0358	–
0.023	–	–	–	2.2720	0.0254	0.0240	0.0518	–
0.0162	–	–	–	1.4040	0.5382	0.0274	0.0620	–
0.0000	–	–	–	2.5885	1.8545	3.1640	0.3300	0.5339
Sum:	0.0030	0.1172	1.7488	29.6959	2.4787	3.3172	0.5524	0.5339

[a]After Usiglio's 1849 work.

The most common evaporite deposits are those rich in calcium sulfate (*anhydrite*, $CaSO_4$; or the hydrated form, *gypsum*, $CaSO_4 \cdot 2H_2O$) and sodium chloride (*halite*). Some deposits also contain magnesium and potassium salts. Evaporite deposits are of great commercial value for these elements.

Other chemical deposits include the oxides of iron and manganese. This includes the "manganese nodules" discovered in great abundance on the deep-ocean floor (Fig. 5-13).

We must not expect to find all sedimentary rocks in the "pure" forms described in this section. Mud and sand are not everywhere clearly separated from each other, nor are muds and calcium carbonate. The mixed sedimentary rocks are called after the dominant component modified by the minor component. For example, a shaly

Figure 5-13 A manganese nodule from the deep ocean floor.

(or "argillaceous" from the French word for mud, *argile*) limestone is a mixture of shale and limestone — a mixture of great economic interest (if the proportions are right) because it is the precursor to cement manufacture.

The range of sedimentary rock types observed in nature is shown in Fig. 5-14.

METAMORPHIC ROCK

We have already implied, in our discussion of granitic rocks, that under the right temperature and pressure conditions a melt of granitic composition could be extracted from a suite of minerals commonly found in sedimentary assemblages. This is the most extreme step in the processes of *metamorphism,* in which a rock is transformed to something other than its original form by increased pressure and temperature.

Some metamorphic rocks are familiar to us in everyday experience. *Marble* is a metamorphosed equivalent of limestone; *slate* is a metamorphic equivalent of shale. Limestone and shale may also undergo more extensive reactions under certain deep-earth conditions.

Metamorphic processes may be classified as *contact* metamorphism, *regional* metamorphism, and *metasomatism.*

Contact Metamorphism

Contact metamorphism occurs where magma heats and recrystallizes the rocks with which it comes into contact. V. M. Goldschmidt, a Norwegian geochemist, in 1911 was able to apply the principles of chemical equilibrium (see Appendix) to the contact metamorphic rocks near Oslo. An inhomogeneous calcareous shale in this region was transformed, at its contact with an intrusive magma, into a rock type called *hornfels.* Pressure and temperature conditions were approximately the same throughout the area, but variations in the composition of the shale resulted in ten

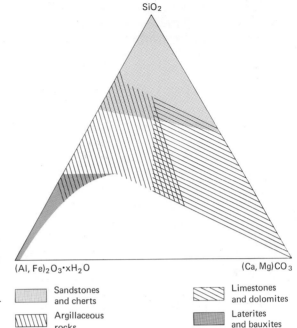

Figure 5-14 The range of composition of sedimentary rocks. After B. Mason, *Principles of Geochemistry* (Third Edition). p 154. Copyright 1966, John Wiley and Sons, Inc.

Sandstones and cherts	Limestones and dolomites
Argillaceous rocks	Laterites and bauxites

different characteristic assemblages in the contact-metamorphosed zone (Fig. 5-15). The temperature and pressure were specified by the magma type and depth of intrusion.

We can use this information to evaluate the petrologically useful generalization from chemical equilibria theory called the *phase rule* (see Appendix) and its applicability to the system. If we lump the similarly behaving magnesium and iron together,

Figure 5-15 Contact metamorphic assemblages in the Oslo region of Norway as deduced by V. M. Goldschmidt. The observed combinations occur either along a line connecting two phases or in a triangle whose corners are three different minerals. Aside from the minerals already discussed in the text the compositions are: *andalusite,* Al_2SiO_5; *cordierite,* Mg_2Al_3 $(AlSi_5O_{18})$; *vesuvianite,* $Ca_{10}Mg_2Al_4(Si_2O_7)_2(SiO_4)_5$- $(OH)_4$; *Wollastonite,* $CaSiO_3$; *hypersthene,* $(Mg, Fe)SiO_3$.

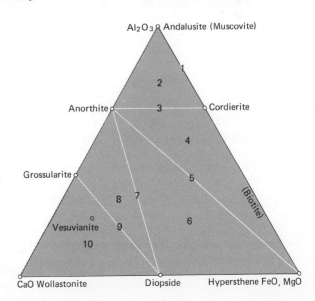

there are five components in these rocks: Al_2O_3, K_2O, SiO_2, CaO, and (Mg,Fe)O. According to the phase rule explained in the Appendix, ϕ (degrees of freedom) = C (number of components) − P (number of phases) + 2 (representing pressure and temperature). We note that in order for the system to be described completely, ϕ must equal zero and, since pressure and temperature are fixed,

$$C = P$$

The components K_2O and SiO_2 may be matched against the observation that two phases, quartz and orthoclase, are present in all the hornfelses. This means that for the *three* remaining components there can be at the most *three* coexisting phases. Goldschmidt found that the hornfelses all along the contact with the intrusive rock had either two or three phases in addition to the quartz and orthoclase, thus fulfilling the phase rule and implying that chemical equilibrium had been attained throughout.

Regional Metamorphism

Regional metamorphism occurs where a vast terrane is subjected to increased pressure and temperature, usually as the result of mountain-building processes.

P. Eskola, a Finnish petrologist, was the first to recognize that different assemblages of minerals in metamorphic rocks were due to large-scale differences in temperature and pressure. We normally take for granted that increases in temperature and pressure represent deeper burial in the earth. There are situations, however, where high temperatures can be produced at shallow depths or a relatively rapid application and release of pressure occurs without as large temperature changes as would be expected in the thermal and pressure gradient.

Figure 5-16 shows the types of rocks expected in regional metamorphism of shale under different temperature and pressure conditions. The different metamorphic states of shale are all lumped together under the name *pelitic* and they define the different metamorphic *grades* or *facies*.

Metasomatism

Metasomatism refers to transformations as the result of significant movement of chemical elements into or out of a rock body. Since all recrystallization involves some movement of chemical species, the term metasomatism is reserved for large-scale effects. These may range from the formation of alternating thin layers of variable composition to the complete alteration of a mass of rock the size of a mountain. The most common species mobilized during metamorphism are water (in the case of clays) and carbon dioxide (in the case of limestones), but other chemicals such as iron, sodium, or potassium also can be shown to undergo large-scale migrations.

One example of metasomatism is the alteration of large, almost pure olivine intrusives by the action of water converting the olivine to a mineral called *serpentine*. The reaction may be written either as:

$$5Mg_2SiO_4 + 4H_2O = 2Mg_3Si_2O_5(OH)_4 + 4MgO + SiO_2$$

$$\text{olivine} \qquad\qquad\qquad \text{serpentine}$$

in which case the metasomatic change in the reaction is clearly the addition of water

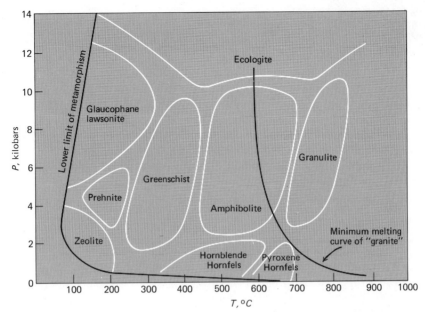

Figure 5-16 Regional metamorphic facies or grades as a function of temperature and pressure. Each facies has a characteristic assemblage of minerals for a given composition. In the case of a pelitic composition the *zeolite*-bearing facies is the lowest pressure and temperature facies encountered. The higher pressure equivalent contains *glaucophane*, $Na_2Mg_3Al_2Si_8O_{22}(OH)_2$, and *lawsonite*, $CaAl_2Si_2O_7(OH)_2 \cdot H_2O$. The greenschist facies is characterized by *chlorite* and *albite*. The hornfels facies are mainly contact metamorphic facies. The amphibolite facies contains a plagioclase ($\sim An_{40}$), *amphibole* assemblage. The granulite facies can have an assemblage typical of igneous rocks and the eclogite facies is characterized by a high-pressure, high-temperature, garnet, pyroxene assemblage. After F. J. Turner, *Metamorphic Petrology,* McGraw-Hill, p. 366, 1968. Copyright 1968. Used by permission of McGraw-Hill Book Co.

and the loss of MgO and SiO_2; or alternatively, in the presence of pyroxene:

$$Mg_2SiO_4 + MgSiO_3 + 2H_2O = Mg_3Si_2O_5(OH)_4$$

olivine   pyroxene   serpentine

where only water is added to the system. The field evidence seems to indicate that the latter metasomatic reaction is the more likely one in most processes of serpentinization.

References

ERNST, W. G., *Earth Materials.* Englewood Cliffs, N.J.: Prentice-Hall, 1969.

VERHOOGEN, J., F. J. TURNER, L. E. WEISS, C. WAHRHAFTIG, and W. S. FYFE, *The Earth: An Introduction to Physical Geology.* New York: Holt, Rinehart and Winston, 1970, 748 pp.

6 The Earth as a Planet

The earth is a member of the solar system and in its makeup, bears significant clues to the general history of planet formation as well as its own peculiar development.

Judging from our recent landings on the moon, the detailed instrumental and photographic exploration of Mars, and the instrumental investigations of Venus, the earth may well be the most complex and interesting planet in our solar system. The earth has an oxygen-rich atmosphere, is 70 percent covered by liquid H_2O and, where land is exposed, it forms patterns of mountains and plains not observed on any other planet.

Add to this a complex planetary interior expressing itself on the surface as earthquakes, volcanoes, deep-sea trenches, and a magnetic field, and we see that the earth's credentials are complete in claiming a large share of our interest during our exploration of the universe.

THE PLANETS

Table 6-1 compares the properties of the planets. The planets are divided into the *inner* or *terrestrial* planets (Mercury, Venus, Earth, Mars) and the *outer* or *Jovian* planets (Jupiter, Saturn, Uranus, Neptune). Pluto is an "oddball" in this scheme, resembling most closely the terrestrial planets though being the remotest of the recorded planets.

The terrestrial planets, the moon, and the moons of the Jovian planets resemble the earth in having high densities and being composed primarily of materials like those found in the meteorites. The Jovian planets are of low density and predominantly composed of solid hydrogen and helium possibly with small cores of meteoritic or terrestrial type material.

Mercury is too close to the sun and too small to have much atmosphere of any sort. The combined effect of the intense heat of the sun and the lack of strong gravitational pull means that most gases will escape rapidly from the surface of Mercury.

Venus is shrouded in an atmosphere of carbon dioxide, with traces of unusual gases, like hydrogen chloride and hydrogen fluoride, but with only small traces of

Table 6-1 Properties of the Planets

	Sun	Mercury	Venus	Earth	Mars	Jupiter	Saturn	Uranus	Neptune	Pluto
Mass (earth = 1)	329,000	0.054	0.81	1[a]	0.11	314	94	14.4	17.0	0.05 ?
Radius (km)	695,000	2439	6050	6370	3400	71,000	57,000	25,800	22,300	2900
Density (g/cm³)	1.41	5.42	5.25	5.52	3.96	1.33	0.68	1.60	1.65	3 ?
Albedo		0.06	0.73	0.39	0.26	0.51	0.50	0.66	0.62	–
Effective temperature (°K)	6000	616	235	240	220	105	75	50	40	40
Surface temperature (°K)		616	600	300	230	130	–	–	–	–
Observed gases in atmosphere	H, He, O, Fe, N, Mg, C, Si, etc.	–	CO_2, H_2O, HCl, HF, O_2(?)	N_2, O_2, Ar, CO_2, H_2O, etc.	CO_2, H_2O	H_2, CH_4, NH_3	H_2, CH_4,	H_2, CH_4,	H_2, CH_4,	–
Distance from the sun (A.U.)[b]		0.39	0.72	1	1.52	5.2	9.5	19.2	30.1	

[a] The mass of the earth is 5.976×10^{27} g.
[b] A.U. = "Astronomic unit" – the mean distance of the earth from the sun (149.6×10^6 km).

water or oxygen. The total quantity of carbon in the atmosphere of Venus is comparable with that in the crust of the earth, where the carbon is locked in shale, limestone, coal, and oil. It almost appears that Venus would have been a twin of the earth had it not had a mysterious history of loss of water and oxygen from the surface.

The major gas on Mars is also carbon dioxide, although the quantity is considerably less than on Venus. The thick carbon dioxide atmosphere on Venus results in a strong heat retention by that planet's atmosphere, resulting in a surface temperature of about 600°K. On Mars, the fact that the total atmosphere is less than 0.01 percent of that of Venus rules out such strong heat-blanketing effects and allows thin carbon dioxide ice ("dry ice") polar caps to condense. Some water is also present on Mars.

The well-rehearsed physical properties of the earth are also gathered together in Table 6-1. These important properties will provide the framework for our more extended description of the planet. For instance, when we compare the average density of the earth (5.5 g/cm³) with the average density of rocks on the earth's surface (3 g/cm³) we realize that the earth's interior must contain a significant amount of denser material to make up the difference.

We will consider first the major features of the earth's surface—features that might be described visually or with the simplest sensors by a spaceman visiting from another planet. Then we shall describe the features of the earth's interior, inferred from results obtained by more sophisticated instrumental observations.

OCEANS AND CONTINENTS

The most obvious thing about the earth's surface is that 71 percent of it is covered by oceans. If we use sea level as a reference, the mean depth of the oceans is about 3800 meters, whereas the mean height of the continents is about 800 meters. The deepest part of the ocean is about 2 km deeper than the highest mountain is high above sea level (Fig. 6-1).

The continents are made up of rocks that, as a whole, are less dense than the rocks of the ocean bottom. As we shall see, this difference maintains the "freeboard" of the continents above the oceans.

At the poles or near them are the Greenland and Antarctic ice caps, survivors of a much more extended ice sheet that was present on earth as late as 11,000 years ago. These ice caps are almost 3000 meters thick at the maximum (Fig. 6-2). If all the ice were to melt, sea level would rise about 60 meters—enough to submerge most coastal cities.

THE ATMOSPHERE

Structure of the Atmosphere

The distribution of gaseous atoms and molecules in the atmosphere is determined by the earth's gravity field and the chemical effects of sunlight on the atoms and molecules. A classification of the major zones of the atmosphere on the basis of temperature is commonly used (Fig. 6-3).

The most obvious feature of the lower atmosphere, or the *troposphere,* is that it

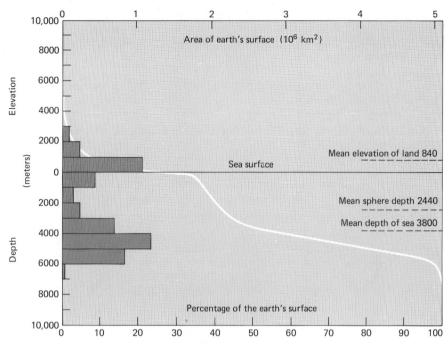

Figure 6-1 The distribution of land elevation and sea depths. After H. V. Sverdrup, M. W. Johnson, and R. H. Fleming, *The Oceans,* Prentice-Hall, 1942.

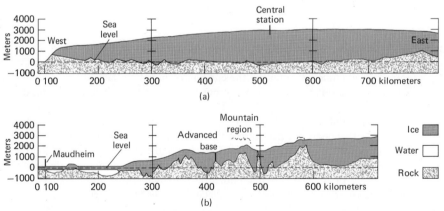

Figure 6-2 Cross section of the (a) Greenland and (b) Antarctic ice caps. *Arctic Research,* Arctic Institute (1956).

becomes more rarified and colder with increasing elevation. The rarification is due to the attenuation of the force of the earth's gravity with distance from the surface. That is, at each level in the atmosphere the differential force on an imaginary parcel of gas is in the upward direction because of the upward decrease in pressure, but it is just matched by the attractive force of gravity downward toward the earth's center. The resultant is the decrease in atmospheric pressure with elevation (Fig. 6-3).

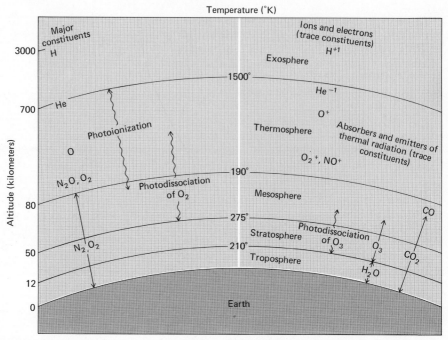

Figure 6-3 The subdivisions of the atmosphere. The pressure at the surface is about 1 *atmosphere*. At 12 km it is about 0.2 atm; at 50 km, 0.001 atm; and at 80 km it is less than 0.0001 atm. Modified from J. C. G. Walker, in *Space/Aeronautics* (1964).

The reason for the temperature decrease with altitude is found in the combined effects of pressure and chemistry. Water and carbon dioxide very effectively absorb infrared radiation reemitted by the earth in response to the sun's rays. In particular, water is the important agent in our atmosphere whereas carbon dioxide predominates on Venus as we noted previously. The absorbed energy is transferred by collisions of the activated water molecules with the major molecular components in the atmosphere. As this energy is transferred it results in movement of the gas molecules, with increased velocity on the average. The faster the molecules move, the higher the temperature of the gas becomes if all other things are maintained the same. Hence the surface of the earth is maintained at a higher temperature than would exist if water vapor or carbon dioxide were absent from the atmosphere.

The amount of water per unit volume decreases with height as does that of all gases. In the troposphere, mixing takes place as a result of this heating. As a hypothetical parcel of air rises, retaining its heat, it expands and cools with the decreased pressure. This results in a decrease in temperature with height. The temperature decrease in the troposphere is about 6.5°K/km (this is called the "lapse rate" and would have been greater in a water-free atmosphere).

If it were not for other strong interactions of sunlight with molecules the lapse rate would give an ever colder atmosphere with height. However other interactions of atmospheric molecules with sunlight *do* occur, thus strongly altering the temperature structure of the atmosphere.

A heat source exists in the vicinity of 50 km because of the optimum absorption of ultraviolet light by ozone (O_3) present at this level. The transfer of heat up and down away from this source results in a gradient of decreasing temperature below and above the 50 km level. Thus the temperature decrease with height observed in the troposphere is reversed and the level of this reversal is called the *tropopause*. The tropopause is at 12 km and has a temperature of 210°K. The region above the tropopause, in which the temperature increases with height, up to 50 km is called the *stratosphere*. Between 50 and 80 km is the *mesosphere*, a transition region of upward decreasing temperature. Above 80-100 km a region of strong heating occurs with increasing altitude due to direct interaction of the sun's rays with the oxygen and nitrogen molecules to produce photodissociation and photoionization. This is called the *thermosphere*. At about 700 km the highest temperature is attained, approximately 1500°K, and the more or less constant high-temperature zone above this height is called the *exosphere*.

Composition of the Atmosphere

In the troposphere, fairly rapid mixing due to convection results in a relatively homogeneous atmosphere except for water which varies with location and season as well as with elevation. The composition of water-free air at sea level is given in Table 6-2.

Nitrogen in the presence of oxygen at the surface of the oceans should combine to form nitrate in solution as the stable form. Both nitrogen and oxygen are maintained at their levels by biological processes.

The argon in the atmosphere is almost completely argon-40, which has been produced by the radioactive decay of potassium-40 in the earth and released to the atmosphere by volcanism and hot-springs activity. Radiogenic argon is released from most minerals at about 300°C, which corresponds to depths in the earth, at the present time, of not much greater than 7 km.

Table 6-2 Composition of Water-Free Air at Sea Level

Component	Content (percent by volume)	Molecular Weight
Nitrogen	78.084	28.0134
Oxygen	20.9476	31.9988
Argon	0.934	39.948
Carbon dioxide	0.0314	44.00995
Neon	0.001818	20.183
Helium	0.000524	4.0026
Krypton	0.000114	83.80
Xenon	0.0000087	131.30
Hydrogen	0.00005	2.01594
Methane	0.0002	16.04303
Nitrous oxide	0.00005	44.0128
Ozone		47.9982
Summer	0 to 0.000007	
Winter	0 to 0.000002	
Sulfur dioxide	0 to 0.0001	64.0628
Nitrogen dioxide	0 to 0.000002	46.0055
Ammonia	0 to trace	17.03061
Carbon monoxide	0 to trace	28.01055
Iodine	0 to 0.000001	253.8088

Table 6-3 Composition of Streams and the Ocean

Atomic Number	Element	Seawater (µg/l)	Streams (µg/l)
1	hydrogen	1.10×10^8	1.10×10^8
2	helium	0.0072	a
3	lithium	170	3
4	beryllium	0.0006	a
5	boron	4450	10
6	carbon (inorganic)	28,000	11,500
	(dissolved organic)	500	a
7	nitrogen (dissolved N_2)	15,000	a
	(as NO_3^{-1}, NO_2^{-1}, NH_4^{+1}		
	and dissolved organic)	670	226
8	oxygen (dissolved O_2)	6000	a
	(as H_2O)	8.83×10^8	8.83×10^8
9	fluorine	1300	100
10	neon	0.120	a
11	sodium	1.08×10^7	6300
12	magnesium	1.29×10^6	4100
13	aluminum	1	400
14	silicon	2900	6100
15	phosphorus	88	20
16	sulfur	9.04×10^5	5600
17	chlorine	1.94×10^7	7800
18	argon	450	a
19	potassium	3.92×10^5	2300
20	calcium	4.11×10^5	15,000
21	scandium	0.0004	0.004
22	titanium	1	3
23	vanadium	1.9	0.9
24	chromium	0.2	1
25	manganese	1.9	7
26	iron	3.4	670
27	cobalt	0.05	0.1
28	nickel	6.6	0.3
29	copper	2	7
30	zinc	2	20
31	gallium	0.03	0.09
32	germanium	0.06	a
33	arsenic	2.6	2
34	selenium	0.090	0.2
35	bromine	67,300	20
36	krypton	0.21	a
37	rubidium	120	1
38	strontium	8100	70
39	yttrium	0.013	0.07
40	zirconium	0.026	a
41	niobium	0.015	a
42	molybdenum	10	0.6
43	technetium	(not naturally occurring)	
44	ruthenium	0.0007	a
45	rhodium	a	a
46	palladium	a	a
47	silver	0.28	0.3
48	cadmium	0.11	a
49	indium	a	a
50	tin	0.81	a
51	antimony	0.33	2
52	tellurium	a	a
53	iodine	64	7
54	xenon	0.47	a

Table 6-3—(continued)

Atomic Number	Element	Seawater (µg/l)	Streams (µg/l)
55	cesium	0.30	0.02
56	barium	21	20
57	lanthanum	0.0034	0.2
58	cerium	0.0012	0.06
59	praseodymium	0.00064	0.03
60	neodymium	0.0028	0.2
61	promethium	(not naturally occurring)	
62	samarium	0.00045	0.03
63	europium	0.000130	0.007
64	gadolinium	0.00070	0.04
65	terbium	0.00014	0.008
66	dysprosium	0.00091	0.05
67	holmium	0.00022	0.01
68	erbium	0.00087	0.05
69	thulium	0.00017	0.009
70	ytterbium	0.00082	0.05
71	lutetium	0.00015	0.008
72	hafnium	<0.008	a
73	tantalum	<0.0025	a
74	tungsten	<0.001	0.03
75	rhenium	0.0084	a
76	osmium	a	a
77	iridium	a	a
78	platinum	a	a
79	gold	0.011	0.002
80	mercury	0.15	0.07
81	thallium	<0.01	a
82	lead	0.03	3
83	bismuth	0.02	a
84–89 and 91	(thorium and uranium decay series elements: polonium, astatine, radon, francium, radium, actinium and protactinium)		
90	thorium	<0.0005	0.1
92	uranium	3.3	0.3

^{a}No data or reasonable estimates available.

Methane and carbon dioxide are closely tied to biological activity. Methane is oxidized to carbon dioxide and water, and its presence is directly sustained by bacterial production.

Also present are the man-made impurities such as sulfur dioxide and carbon monoxide, whose high concentrations in urban areas is responsible for the physical discomforts of smog.

THE HYDROSPHERE

The realm of water is dominated by the vast oceans on our planet. Ninety-eight percent of the water on the earth's surface is in the oceans, the remaining 2 percent being distributed among lakes, rivers, glaciers, groundwater, and atmospheric water.

Seawater has about 3.5 percent dissolved salts (mainly sodium chloride), whereas streams average about 0.012 percent (or 120 parts per million). The salt content of water is called its *salinity*. The compositions of streams and the ocean are given in Table 6-3.

Table 6-4   Water Balance Between Streams and Oceans

	Water Balance	
	$g \cdot cm^{-2} \cdot yr^{-1}$	$10^{20} g \cdot yr^{-1}$
Evaporation from ocean surfaces	106	3.83
Precipitation on ocean surfaces	96	3.47
Evaporation from land surfaces	42	0.63
Precipitation on land surfaces	67	0.99
Run-off to oceans	10	0.36

The total flow of water to the oceans via streams is about 3.6×10^{16} liters per year. Inasmuch as the surface area of the oceans is about 3.6×10^{18} cm², this means that 10 liters of river water is added to every square centimeter of ocean surface every thousand years. There are 400 liters of seawater in a 4000-meter column in the ocean with a cross-sectional area of 1 cm²; hence it would take 40,000 years to fill the ocean basins with stream water if none of it were recycled through evaporation and precipitation. Since we know that the only significant source of water in streams is derived from the oceans through evaporation and precipitation, this age is not a true "filling up" age. Rather, it indicates that a water molecule spends an average length of time of 40,000 years in the ocean before it is evaporated and recycled. The water balance between the continents and the oceans is presented in Table 6-4. The oceans circulate on a much shorter time scale than 40,000 years, so the salinity of the open ocean does not vary greatly from place to place even though evaporation or freshwater dilution is pronounced in some areas. (These small differences are nevertheless important in ocean circulation processes.)

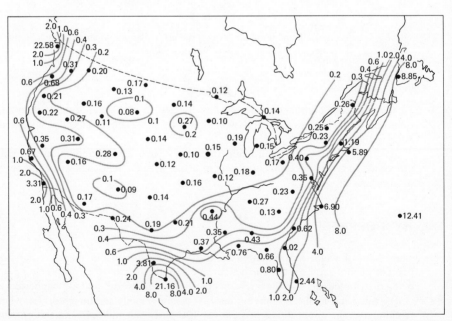

Figure 6-4   The chloride concentration distribution in rains, showing the effect of marine aerosols at the continental boundaries. C. Junge and W. Werbe, Journal of Meteorology, 15, 417 (1958). By permission of the American Meteorological Society.

The composition of streams (Table 6-3) is controlled by the contributions from weathering and deposition from atmospheric precipitation. High sodium chloride concentrations are seen in rains in maritime areas of continents and in islands (Fig. 6-4). The salt grains from sea spray form an *aerosol*. These grains act as nucleation sites for the formation of raindrops. Many of the aerosol particles impact directly on trees during dry times and are washed out by the next rain. As a result it has been found that the total flux of aerosols to the stream load is three times the flux determined from the concentration of salts in rain.

The factors that control the composition of seawater are diverse and complex. As we saw in Chapter 5, some sediments are formed by the extraction of compounds from seawater either biologically or chemically. This process tends to keep up with the supply of dissolved material to the oceans, thus keeping the concentrations of calcium and silicon, for example, constant with time in seawater.

The surface waters of the open sea are efficiently aerated. At high latitudes the surface waters are injected deep into the oceans by the large-scale circulation pat-

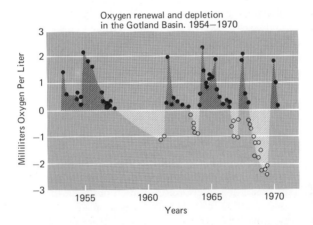

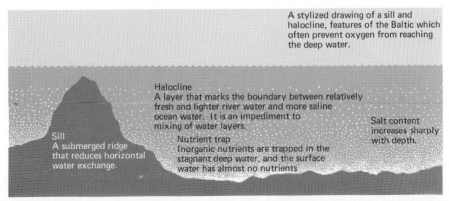

Figure 6-5 The structure of a portion of the Baltic Sea, which becomes anaerobic because the rate of organic debris oxidation exceeds the rate of supply of oxygenated water. From S. H. Fonselius, *Environment*, **12**, 2 (1970). Reprinted by permission of and Copyright 1970 by Committee for Environmental Information, Inc.

terns of the oceans. There a slow oxidation of organic material by biological processes tends to decrease the dissolved oxygen. Long before the oxygen is exhausted the circulation of the oceans has brought the water in contact with the atmosphere again. In restricted basins, such as the Black Sea and the Baltic Sea, biological decay of falling plankton consumes oxygen in the deeper parts of the water column more rapidly than the water can be aerated (Fig. 6-5). At depth in the Black Sea and occasionally in the Baltic Sea (Fig 6-5), dissolved oxygen gives way to dissolved hydrogen sulfide produced by anaerobic sulfate-reducing bacteria. (The same thing happens in sediments containing a high concentration of degradable organic matter. The waters in the pores of the sediment quickly lose their dissolved oxygen through the action of aerobic organisms and then the anaerobic process begins to operate. The strong "rotten egg" odor of hydrogen sulfide gas can often be detected around marine mud flats at low tide due to this process.) The process seems to be accelerating in many water bodies because of human pollution.

In natural aqueous systems the role of carbon dioxide in determining the acidity or the basicity of the water is very important. If we consider pure water as neutral we will find that rainwater is slightly acid because of dissolved carbon dioxide (CO_2) from air. Soil waters are even more acidic because of the carbon dioxide from plant respiration and decay. In seawater the dissolved carbon dioxide from the atmosphere can react with the precipitated calcium carbonate and when it does the result is a slightly basic solution. This solution is maintained in that condition becoming neither more strongly acid nor more strongly basic by a "buffering" action due to the presence of solid $CaCO_3$, gaseous and dissolved CO_2, and the ions Ca^{+2}, CO_3^{-2}, and HCO_3^{-1}, H^{+1}, and OH^{-1} in addition to the water in which they all occur.

THE INTERIOR OF THE EARTH

Let us now probe what lies below the surface of the earth. There are two lines of evidence concerning the interior constitution of the earth. The first is the mean density of the earth relative to surface rocks and the second is the information derived from the way in which earthquake waves are transmitted through the earth.

Mass Distribution

As already mentioned, material at depth in the earth must be of higher density than surface material.

Some of this increased density can be ascribed to the changes that take place in the silicate minerals (Table 6-5). Olivine, with a density of 3 g/cm^3, is transformed at a depth of about 700 km (as a result of the increased pressure) to another polymorph, a mineral belonging to the *spinel* family, with a density of about 3.6 g/cm^3, much as graphite can be converted to diamond. At even greater depths, other pressure-dependent phase transformations may take place.

Despite all these increases in density of silicate materials, the average density of the earth is not accounted for by this process alone. An even denser phase is required, such as metallic iron-nickel alloy, which we know to be a good candidate on the basis of cosmic elemental abundance and studies of meteorites. Because of its greater-than-silicate density, this material would be expected to settle out as the core of the earth.

Table 6-5   Densities of Some Typical Minerals

Mineral	Composition	Density (g/cm³)
graphite	C	2.27
diamond	C	3.52
quartz	SiO_2	2.65
coesite	SiO_2	2.91
stishovite	SiO_2	4.29
almandite (garnet)	$Fe_3Al_2Si_3O_{12}$	4.32
enstatite (pyroxene)	$MgSiO_3$	3.20
forsterite (olivine)	Mg_2SiO_4	3.21
spinel	$MgAl_2O_4$	3.58
magnetite	$FeFe_2O_4$	5.21
jadeite	$NaAlSi_2O_6$	3.32
albite (feldspar)	$NaAlSi_3O_8$	2.62

Earthquakes and the Structure of the Earth's Interior

Earthquake waves give us further valuable information about the nature of the phase distributions in the earth's interior. The study of earthquake waves is called *seismology.*

When an earthquake occurs, energy waves resembling sound waves are transmitted away from the site or *focus* of the earthquake (Fig. 6-6). (The place on the earth's surface directly above the focus is called the *epicenter.*) The path of the waves is shown in Fig. 6-6. Generally, with increasing depth, because of pressure-dependent changes in the transmissive properties of the interior, the velocity of the waves increases. The resulting refraction gives the arcuate paths shown in the figure. *Seismographs,* detecting instruments placed at various points on the surface, will receive the *first arrival* of earthquake waves at different times depending on their locations.

At a specific distance away from the focus of the earthquake, namely between 105° to 142° along the arc of a great circle drawn through the epicenter, these first strong impulse earthquake waves are not recorded (Fig. 6-6). This marked disappearance of an expected signal suggests that a phase boundary has been encoun-

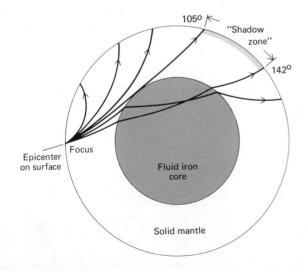

Figure 6-6   The path of earthquake rays and the inferred interior structure of the earth. Because of the scale of the figure the focus cannot be distinguished from the epicenter.

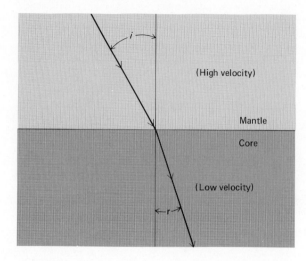

Figure 6-7 An example of refraction at a phase boundary of the type at the core-mantle boundary. The angle of incidence is smaller than the angle of refraction.

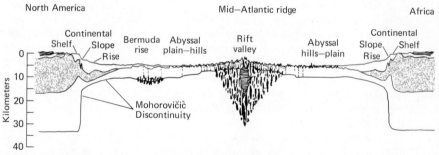

Figure 6-8 The Mohorovicic discontinuity under the continents and the oceans—a section across the Atlantic Ocean. From B. C. Heezen, M. Tharp, and M. Ewing, The Geological Society of America, Special Paper 65 (1959).

Table 6-6 Major Subdivisions of the Earth

Unit	Depth (km)	Mass (× 10²⁴ grams)	Volume (× 10¹⁰ km³)	Density (g/cm³)	Percent Mass of Earth
Crust					
continental	0–40	16			
seawater	0–4	1.4			
oceanic	4–11	7.0			
average		25	0.9	2.8	0.4
Mantle	25–2900	4075	89.4	3.5 increasing with depth to 6.5	68.2
Core	2900–6370	1880	18	9.5 increasing with depth to 13.5	31.4
Earth		5980	108.3	5.517	100.0

tered by the wave at great depth. This boundary, or *discontinuity*, is inferred to be the demarcation of the iron-nickel *core* and the silicate *mantle* (as the silicate portion below the crust is called). A very strong wave refraction has occurred because the waves have passed from the mantle, where they traveled at a relatively high velocity, into the core, where they traveled at a relatively low velocity (Fig. 6-7).

Table 6-7   A Possible Composition of the Upper Mantle[a]

Component	Model Pyrolite (percent)	Component	Model Pyrolite (percent)
SiO_2	45.16	Cr_2O_3	0.43
MgO	37.49	NiO	0.20
FeO	8.04	CoO	0.01
Fe_2O_3	0.46	TiO_2	0.71
Al_2O_3	3.54	MnO	0.14
CaO	3.08	P_2O_5	0.06
Na_2O	0.57		
K_2O	0.13		100.00

[a]After A. E. Ringwood.

The boundary between the crust and the mantle is also a sharp discontinuity based primarily on compositional differences between the two units. The crust-mantle boundary, called the *Mohorovičić discontinuity,* is deeper under mountain roots in particular and under continents generally, and is shallower under the deep-ocean basins (Fig. 6-8).

Table 6-6 shows the major units of the earth, their boundary locations, and mass.

The Mantle

We do not have a highly refined idea of the composition of the mantle. Apparently the upper mantle is in a more oxidized state than the lower mantle because the volcanic rocks tapping the upper mantle have a higher degree of oxidized iron (Fe^{+3}) than would be permitted if an iron-nickel core were in equilibrium with it.

Rocks derived from the mantle are not exact chemical replicas of the mantle but rather represent the fraction that can be melted from the mantle rocks.

What then can we say about the composition of the mantle? It is primarily magnesium and iron silicate, with some sodium, calcium, potassium, and aluminum. The rock of the upper mantle has been called *pyrolite,* because such a composition could be constructed using the proper proportions of pyroxene and olivine. Table 6-7 gives the composition of pyrolite that would fit the requirements at least for upper mantle composition.

The Crust

The average composition of major units of the earth's crust are presented in Table 6-8. For the sake of arriving at some idea of the average crustal composition we tend to use the compositions of the major rock types found at the surface. The uncertainty in doing this is that we only have inferential evidence concerning what we should expect if we looked 20 or 30 km below the surface. Realizing these uncertainties

Table 6-8 Distribution of Elements in the Crust of Earth (Concentrations in Parts per Million)*

| | Igneous Rocks | | Granitic Rocks | | | Sedimentary Rocks | | | Crustal Abundance | |
Element	Ultramafic	Basaltic	High Ca	Low Ca	Syenites	Shales	Sandstones	Carbonates	Model A	Model B
1 Hydrogen H		See note a					See note a		See note a	
2 Helium He		See note b					See note b		See note b	
3 Lithium Li	0.X**	17.	24.	40.	28.	66.	15.	5.	29.	20.
4 Beryllium Be	0.X	1.	2.	3.	1.	3.	0.X	0.X	2.	2.
5 Boron B	3.	5.	9.	10.	9.	100.	35.	20.	9.	7.
6 Carbon C		See note a					See note a		See note a	
7 Nitrogen N	6.	20.	20.	20.	30.		See note a		20.	20.
8 Oxygen O		See note a					See note a		See note a	
9 Fluorine F	100.	400.	520.	850.	1,200.	740.	270.	330.	650.	460.
10 Neon Ne		See note b					See note b		See note b	
11 Sodium Na	4,200.	18,000.	28,400.	25,800.	40,400.	9,600.	3,300.	400.	31,900.	23,200.
12 Magnesium Mg	204,000.	46,000.	9,400.	1,600.	5,800.	15,000.	7,000.	47,000.	33,000.	27,700.
13 Aluminum Al	20,000.	78,000.	82,000.	72,000.	88,000.	80,000.	25,000.	4,200.	77,400.	80,000.
14 Silicon Si	205,000.	230,000.	314,000.	347,000.	291,000.	273,000.	368,000.	24,000.	311,000.	272,000.
15 Phosphorus P	220.	1,100.	920.	600.	800.	700.	170.	400.	820.	1,010.
16 Sulfur S	300.	300.	300.	300.	300.	2,400.	240.	1,200.	300.	300.
17 Chlorine Cl	100.	60.	130.	200.	430.	180.	20.	365.	210.	190.
18 Argon Ar									See note d	
19 Potassium K	34.	8,300.	25,200.	42,000.	48,000.	26,600.	10,700.	2,700.	29,500.	16,800.
20 Calcium Ca	25,000.	76,000.	25,300.	5,100.	18,000.	22,100.	39,100.	302,300.	25,700.	50,600.
21 Scandium Sc	16.	30.	14.	7.	3.	13.	1.	1.	14.	22.
22 Titanium Ti	300.	13,800.	3,400.	1,200.	3,500.	4,600.	1,500.	400.	4,400.	8,600.
23 Vanadium V	40.	250.	88.	44.	30.	130.	20.	20.	98.	170.
24 Chromium Cr	2,980.	170.	22.	4.1	2.	90.	35.	11.	48.	96.
25 Manganese Mn	1,040.	1,500.	540.	390.	850.	850.	X0.	1,100.	670.	1,000.
26 Iron Fe	94,300.	86,500.	29,600.	14,200.	36,700.	47,200.	9,800.	3,800.	34,300.	58,000.
27 Cobalt Co	110.	48.	7.	1.	1.	19.	0.33	0.1	12.	28.
28 Nickel Ni	2,000.	130.	15.	4.5	4.	68.	2.	20.	37.	72.
29 Copper Cu	10.	87.	30.	10.	5.	45.	X.	4.	32.	58.
30 Zinc Zn	50.	105.	60.	39.	130.	95.	16.	20.	63.	82.
31 Gallium Ga	1.5	17.	17.	17.	30.	19.	12.	4.	18.	17.
32 Germanium Ge	1.5	1.5	1.3	1.3	1.	1.6	0.8	0.2	1.3	1.3
33 Arsenic As	1.	2.	1.9	1.5	1.4	13.	1.	1.	1.7	2.0
34 Selenium Se	0.05	0.05	0.05	0.05	0.05	0.6	0.05	0.08	0.05	0.05
35 Bromine Br	1.	3.6	4.5	1.3	2.7	4.	1.	6.2	3.0	4.0
36 Krypton Kr		See note b					See note b		See note b	
37 Rubidium Rb	0.13	30.	110.	170.	110.	140.	60.	3.	120.	70.
38 Strontium Sr	5.8	465.	440.	100.	200.	300.	20.	610.	300.	450.
39 Yttrium Y	5.0	25.	44.	41.	14.	35.	10.	4.3	38.	35.
40 Zirconium Zr	45.	140.	140.	175.	500.	160.	220.	19.	170.	140.
41 Niobium Nb	16.	19.	20.	21.	35.	11.	0.0X	0.3	21.	20.
42 Molybdenum Mo	0.3	1.5	1.0	1.3	0.6	2.6	0.2	0.4	1.2	1.2
43 Technetium Tc	See note c	See note c					See note c		See note c	
44 Ruthenium Ru	See note d	See note d					See note d		See note d	
45 Rhodium Rh	See note d	See note d					See note d		See note d	
46 Palladium Pd	0.012	0.005	0.00X	0.00X			See note d		0.002	0.003
47 Silver Ag	0.06	0.11	0.051	0.037	See note d	0.07	See note d	0.0X	0.06	0.08
48 Cadmium Cd	0.03	0.22	0.13	0.13	0.0X	0.3	0.0X	0.035	0.15	0.18
49 Indium In	0.01	0.22	0.26	0.26	0.13	0.1	0.0X	0.0X	0.2	0.2
50 Tin Sn	0.5	1.5	1.5	3.	X.	6.0	0.X	0.X	2.1	1.5
51 Antimony Sb	0.5	0.12	0.2	0.2	2.2	1.5	0.4	0.2	0.3	0.2
52 Tellurium Te	See note d	See note d					See note d		See note d	

Abundance of the elements (values in ppm unless otherwise noted)*

| | Igneous Rocks | | | | | Sedimentary Rocks | | | Crustal Abundance | |
| | | | Granitic Rocks | | | | | | | |
Element	Ultramafic	Basaltic	High Ca	Low Ca	Syenites	Shales	Sandstones	Carbonates	Model A	Model B
53 Iodine I	0.5	0.5	0.5	0.5	0.5	2.2	1.7	1.2	0.5	0.5
54 Xenon Xe		See note b					See note b		See note b	
55 Cesium Cs	0.X	1.1	2.	4.	0.6	6.	X.0	6.	3.1	1.6
56 Barium Ba	0.4	330.	420.	840.	1,600.	580.	X0.	10.	610.	380.
57 Lanthanum La	4.5	17.	84.	55.	20.	39.	7.2	3.7	58.	50.
58 Cerium Ce	9.3	66.	100.	57.	30.	76.	15.	8.0	74.	83.
59 Praseodymium Pr	1.8	8.5	17.	7.2	5.2	10.	2.1	1.2	11.	13.
60 Neodymium Nd	6.2	32.	55.	33.	19.	37.	8.8	3.3	41.	44.
61 Promethium Pm	See note c	See note c	See note c	See note c	See note c	See note c	See note c	See note c	See note c	See note c
62 Samarium Sm	1.1	6.9	8.5	7.1	2.7	7.0	1.9	0.61	7.4	7.7
63 Europium Eu	0.32	2.7	1.7	1.1	0.88	2.0	0.51	0.12	1.6	2.2
64 Gadolinium Gd	1.2	5.9	6.7	7.1	2.7	6.1	1.8	0.61	6.6	6.3
65 Terbium Tb	0.31	1.1	1.0	1.3	0.48	1.3	0.38	0.07	1.1	1.0
66 Dysprosium Dy	1.3	9.0	8.0	5.0	2.0	4.6	1.4	0.60	6.8	8.5
67 Holmium Ho	0.18	1.1	2.2	1.2	0.46	1.2	0.35	0.24	1.5	1.6
68 Erbium Er	0.53	3.3	3.8	4.4	1.8	4.0	1.1	0.30	3.9	3.6
69 Thulium Tm	0.068	0.44	0.6	0.68	0.27	0.58	0.36	0.058	0.59	0.52
70 Ytterbium Yb	0.50	2.7	4.0	4.0	1.5	3.4	0.85	0.41	3.7	3.4
71 Lutetium Lu	0.072	0.5	1.1	1.2	0.27	0.60	0.063	0.067	1.0	0.8
72 Hafnium Hf	0.6	6.	2.3	3.9	11.	2.8	3.9	0.3	4.	4.
73 Tantalum Ta	1.0	1.1	3.6	4.2	2.1	0.8	0.0X	0.0X	3.3	2.4
74 Tungsten W	0.77	0.7	1.3	2.2	1.33	1.8	1.6	0.6	1.5	1.0
75 Rhenium Re	See note d	0.0006	0.000X	0.0006	0.0003	0.0005	0.0003	0.000X	0.0004	0.0004
76 Osmium Os	See note d	0.0005	0.0000X	0.00004	0.0000X	See note d	See note d		0.0001	0.0002
77 Iridium Ir	See note d	0.0003	0.0000X	0.00007	0.0000X	See note d	See note d		0.00009	0.0002
78 Platinum Pt	See note d	See note d	See note d		See note d	See note d	See note d		See note d	See note d
79 Gold Au	0.002	0.002	0.002	0.002	0.002	0.005	0.006	0.006	0.002	0.002
80 Mercury Hg	0.004	0.01	0.02	0.04	0.0X	0.4	0.03	0.04	0.03	0.02
81 Thallium Tl	0.06	0.21	0.72	2.3	1.4	1.4	0.82	0.0X	1.3	0.47
82 Lead Pb	1.	6.	15.	19.	12.	20.	7.	9.	15.	10.
83 Bismuth Bi	See note d	See note d	See note d	0.01	See note d	See note d	See note d	See note d	0.005	0.004
84 Polonium Po	See note e	See note e	See note e	See note e	See note e	See note e	See note e	See note e	See note e	See note e
85 Astatine At	See note e	See note e	See note e	See note e	See note e	See note e	See note e	See note e	See note e	See note e
86 Radon Rn	See note e	See note e	See note e	See note e	See note e	See note e	See note e	See note e	See note e	See note e
87 Francium Fr	See note e	See note e	See note e	See note e	See note e	See note e	See note e	See note e	See note e	See note e
88 Radium Ra	See note e	See note e	See note e	See note e	See note e	See note e	See note e	See note e	See note e	See note e
89 Actinium Ac	See note e	See note e	See note e	See note e	See note e	See note e	See note e	See note e	See note e	See note e
90 Thorium Th	0.004	2.7	8.9	20.	13.	12.	5.5	1.7	12.	5.8
91 Protactinium Pa	See note e	See note e	See note e	See note e	See note e	See note e	See note e	See note e	See note e	See note e
92 Uranium U	0.001	0.9	2.3	4.7	3.0	3.7	1.7	2.2	2.9	1.6
93 Neptunium Np	See note f	See note f	See note f	See note f	See note f	See note f	See note f	See note f	See note f	See note f
94 Plutonium Pu	See note f	See note f	See note f	See note f	See note f	See note f	See note f	See note f	See note f	See note f

*From K. K. Turekian in Encyclopedia of Science and Technology, Second Edition (McGraw-Hill, 1971).

**X, 0.X, and the like indicate order of magnitude known. Model A crustal abundance: 0.25% ultramafic rocks, 18% basaltic rocks, 39% high-calcium granitic rocks, 39% low calcium-granitic rocks, and 3.75% syenites. Model B crustal abundance: 50% basaltic rocks and 50% high-calcium granitic rocks.

[a] The elements hydrogen, carbon, nitrogen, and oxygen are the basic constituents of the biosphere, hydrosphere, and atmosphere. Oxygen is also the most important element of the lithosphere while carbon is important in sedimentary rocks.

[b] The rare gases occur in the atmosphere in the following amounts (% vol): helium, 0.00052; neon, 0.0018; argon, 0.93; krypton, 0.00011; and xenon, 0.0000087. Helium is produced by radioactive decay of uranium and thorium but is also lost to outer space. Argon-40 is produced by the radioactive decay of potassium-40 and is the major isotope of argon in the atmosphere. Owing to the effect of radioactive decay, the argon and helium contents of rocks vary with the age of the rocks. The estimated rare-gas contents of igneous rocks are (at standard temperature and pressure in ml/g of rock): He, 6×10^{-5}; Ne, 7.7×10^{-8}; Ar, 2.2×10^{-5}; Kr, 4.2×10^{-9}; and Xe, 3.4×10^{-10}.

[c] The elements technetium and promethium do not occur naturally in the earth's crust.

[d] Data for these are missing or unreliable.

[e] The following elements are present only as radioactive daughters of the long-lived radioactive parents uranium and thorium: polonium, astatine, radon, francium, radium, actinium, and protactinium.

[f] The elements neptunium and plutonium occur naturally only as a consequence of neutron capture by uranium.

we can make a rough estimate of average crustal composition by considering the two most abundant rock types, the high-calcium granitic rocks and the basalts. The last column of Table 6-8 is the average of one part high-calcium granitic rock and one part basalt.

References

ABELL, G., *Exploration of the Universe.* New York: Holt, Rinehart and Winston, 1969 (2nd ed.), 772 pp.

CLARK, S. P., JR., *Earth Structure.* Englewood Cliffs, N.J.: Prentice-Hall, 1971, 136 pp. Available in paperback.

GOODY, R. M. and J. C. G. WALKER, *Atmospheres,* Englewood Cliffs, N.J.: Prentice-Hall, 1972, 160 pp. Available in paperback.

GORDON, R. B., *Physics of the Earth.* New York: Holt, Rinehart and Winston, 1972, 180 pp. Available in paperback.

JACOBS, J. A., R. D. RUSSELL, and J. T. WILSON, *Physics and Geology.* New York: McGraw-Hill, 1959, 424 pp.

TUREKIAN, K. K., *Oceans,* Englewood Cliffs, N.J.: Prentice-Hall, 1968, 120 pp. Available in paperback.

7 The Radioactivity Clock

Perhaps one of the most exciting applications of the principles of chemistry and physics to the study of the earth and the solar system has been the use of radioactivity to determine geologic time. The measurement of time is as critical for the scientist in understanding the history of the planets as it is to the seaman using celestial or satellite navigation to determine location accurately. It is the systematic nature of the radioactive "decay" law that gives it the qualities of a clock. In this chapter we will explore this law and its application to such problems as the age of the earth, the ages of mountain building, the time scale of evolution, and the rates of oceanic processes.

THE RADIOACTIVE DECAY LAW

We saw in Chapter 2 that some nuclides are unstable or radioactive, and reach more stable states by the emission of alpha, beta, and gamma particles. These energetic particles are the result of transformations within the nucleus itself, not the result of collisions or interactions of the nucleus with other nuclei.

Although we can identify which nuclides are radioactive, we cannot predict exactly when any one nucleus will undergo its transformation. Instead we must treat the behavior of a large assemblage of nuclei in a statistical manner. When we do this we come out with the fundamental law of radioactive decay: *The number of radioactive nuclei that decay in a unit time interval is directly proportional to the number of nuclei present at that instant.* This law has been verified without exception for every radioactive nuclide studied, and is expressed in mathematical shorthand as

$$\frac{\Delta N}{\Delta t} = -\lambda N$$

where $\Delta N / \Delta t$ is the rate of change with time (Δ is the Greek capital "delta" and means "difference in") in the number N of radioactive nuclei present at that instant, and λ is the *decay constant,* the proportionality constant relating the rate of change to the number of nuclei present. It is a unique value for each radioactive nuclide.

The negative sign indicates that the size of N is diminishing with time because of the decay. This equation when written in the proper mathematical form instead of the simple form expressed above can be used to follow the value of N as t increases. The resulting equation is

$$N = N_0 e^{-\lambda t}$$

This equation indicates that if we start with a number of radioactive particles N_0 at some time that we designate as time zero, after a length of time t has elapsed the number of particles still remaining is N.

This type of mathematical expression describes an *exponential decrease* and the base of the exponential scale is the so-called "natural base" e. The value of e is 2.718. Tables of logarithms to the base e are readily available or a simple conversion from base-e logarithm to base-10 logarithm can be performed in the following way:

$$\log_e X = 2.303 \, \log_{10} X$$

Often, to avoid subscripts, $\log_{10}$ is written simply as log, and $\log_e$ is written ln. Hence the above equation could be written:

$$\ln X = 2.303 \, \log X$$

If we take the natural logarithm (base e) of the integrated form of the radioactive decay equation we get

$$\ln N = \ln N_0 - \lambda t$$

or

$$2.303 \, \log N = 2.303 \, \log N_0 - \lambda t$$

Hence a plot of the logarithm (either to the base e or base 10) against time will give a straight line (Fig. 7-1). The slope of the line is λ for the base-e plot and $\lambda/2.303$ for the base-10 plot.

Sometimes another index of the decay constant is used: the *half-life,* which is the length of time required to diminish the original number of radioactive nuclei by half. By using the above equation it can be shown that the decay constant is related to the half-life ($t_{1/2}$) by the equality $t_{1/2} = 0.693/\lambda$.

PRINCIPLES OF RADIOACTIVE DATING

Types of Radioactive Species Used in Dating

How were the various types of natural radioactive nuclides formed? We can group the naturally occurring radioactive nuclides into categories related to their origin and survival: primary, secondary, relict, and cosmogenic (Table 7-1). The *primary* radioactive nuclides were created in the galaxy prior to the formation of the solar system and, because of their long half-lives, are still present. *Secondary* nuclides are the radioactive daughters of the heavier primary nuclides, uranium and thorium. Secondary nuclides exist despite their short half-lives only because they are being con-

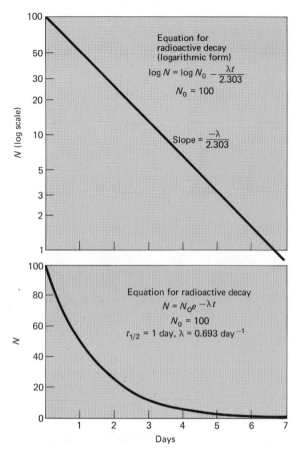

Figure 7-1 The radioactive decay curve. The radioactive nuclide that is decaying is called the *parent* and the nuclide that is formed by the decay is called the *daughter*. The daughter itself may be radioactive in which case it becomes the parent to the next nuclide in the series. Starting with N_0 atoms of a radioactive nuclide decaying to a stable daughter, after time t, N will be the number of parent nuclei remaining and N_0-N will be the number of daughter nuclei formed.

tinuously generated. *Relict* nuclides are short-lived primary nuclides that have left an indelible trace on material formed from the condensing solar system. The "remains" may be expressed today in the form of the anomalously high abundance of a nuclide such as ^{129}Xe in some meteorites produced from now extinct ^{129}I, or other isotopes of the rare gases produced by fission of extinct elements heavier than ura-

Table 7-1 Categories of Radioactive Nuclides Suitable for Dating

Category	Nuclides	Chronometric Uses
1. Primary	^{235}U, ^{238}U, ^{232}Th, ^{40}K, ^{87}Rb, ^{187}Re	Rocks, meteorites, shells
2. Secondary	^{234}U, ^{230}Th, ^{226}Ra, ^{210}Pb, ^{231}Pa	Deep-sea sediments, ocean water, glacial ice, corals, travertines.
3. Cosmic-ray induced	^{14}C, ^{3}H, ^{32}Si, ^{10}Be, ^{7}Be	Wood, bones, shells, ancient smelted iron, deep-sea sediments, ocean water
4. Relict	^{129}I, ^{244}Pu	Age of early events in the solar system, chronology of the universe

nium or in the form of fission tracks left in solid crystals. *Cosmogenic* nuclides are produced by the incessant bombardment of the planets by galactic cosmic rays. In our atmosphere such reactions produce, among other nuclides, carbon-14, a remarkably useful nuclide in the study of recent events.

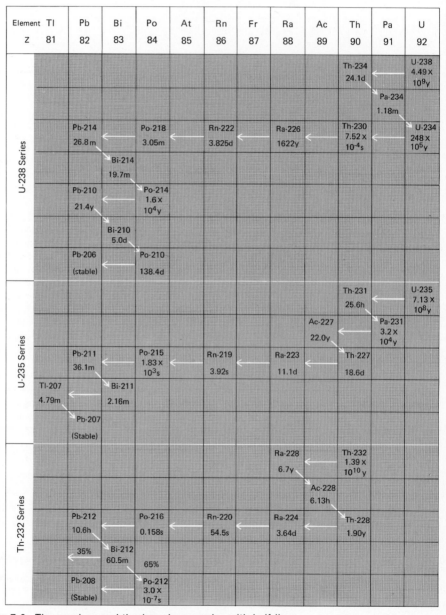

Figure 7-2 The uranium and thorium decay series with half-lives.

Secular Equilibrium

The primary radioactive nuclides ^{235}U, ^{238}U, and ^{232}Th decay through a series of radioactive daughters, which we have called secondary radioactive nuclides, to their stable lead isotopes ^{207}Pb, ^{206}Pb, and ^{208}Pb, respectively (Fig. 7-2). Because the primary parent has by far the longest half-life in the series, a steady condition called *secular equilibrium* is eventually established in which the rate of decay of each secondary nuclide in the chain is forced to be the same as the decay rate of primary uranium or thorium. If the system is chemically disturbed (for instance if we "suddenly" extract all the secondary nuclides from the uranium), the system will recover toward secular equilibrium once again. The time scale for this recovery is about five times the half-life of the longest lived daughter in the decay chain. Of the three decay series, ^{238}U takes the longest to return to secular equilibrium – about one million years. The readjustment is itself a "clock," which is extremely useful for dating short-term events.

Requirements for Dating

So far we have been talking in generalities. It does not follow, however, that we can make a simple application of these concepts without some precautions.

Consider, as a simple case, the decay of carbon-14. In principle we can calculate an age by comparing the amount of ^{14}C remaining today with the original amount. The equation is

$$2.303 \log N = 2.303 \log N_0 - \lambda t$$

In order to make use of this equation, we must know the value of N_0, the original amount. This is of course not possible to obtain directly since there is no indication of N_0 implicit in our measurement. We must therefore create a model to enable us to estimate N_0; accuracy of dating will depend on the validity of our model.

A second requirement of all radioactive dating schemes is that a piece of wood, a mineral, or a rock that is a candidate for dating must not have received new radioactive (or *parent*, Fig. 7-1) nuclei or lost any that it once possessed (except through radioactive decay). Only in the case of the uranium decay series where two uranium isotopes are decaying to two different *daughter* isotopes of lead at different rates is it possible to detect a failure of this assumption positively.

A third requirement refers to dating techniques in which the present-day ratio of daughter residue to parent is used as an index of time. This applies to the primary radioactive nuclides, such as ^{40}K, ^{87}Rb, ^{235}U, ^{238}U, and ^{232}Th, and their respective daughters ^{40}Ar, ^{87}Sr, ^{207}Pb, ^{206}Pb, and ^{208}Pb.

Starting with an earlier expression,

$$N = N_0 e^{-\lambda t}$$

it is obvious that after a length of time t has elapsed there are N atoms of the parent left and the remainder, $N_0 - N$, is present in the form of a daughter. Rearranging the equation, we get

$$N_0 = N e^{\lambda t}$$

Subtracting N from both sides,

$$N_0 - N = N \, (e^{\lambda t} - 1)$$

and dividing through by N, we obtain

$$\frac{N_0 - N}{N} = e^{\lambda t} - 1$$

$N_0 - N$ may be designated d, the number of daughter atoms present today, and N may be designated p, the number of parent atoms remaining today. We can re-write the above expression explicitly in terms of time:

$$\frac{2.303}{\lambda} \log \left(\frac{d}{p} + 1 \right) = t$$

It is obvious that in this case not only must the criterion of no loss or gain of parent be met but also a similar criterion is required for the daughter. Attempts are made to rescue information on systems where loss of the daughter seemingly has occurred, but these corrections are usually less than ideal.

The fourth requirement is that a method must be devised to correct for "background" contamination — the presence of daughter nuclide atoms not produced on the spot by radioactive decay. Because most of the elements that are represented by the radiogenic nuclide also have other nonradiogenic isotopes, a subtraction of the contaminant can often be made.

THE APPLICATION OF RADIOACTIVE DATING

Now that we have familiarized ourselves with the basic principles of radioactive dating (or *geochronometry*, as it has come to be called), let us next discuss how we may solve some fundamental problems of time and sequence in the history of man and his planet.

The Age of the Solar System

The earth is not a reliable source of information for its own age or that of the solar system. The surface of the earth, from which rocks are obtained, has been reprocessed again and again; it retains a "memory" of its own history only from about 3.5 billion years ago to the present.

Until we landed on the moon, our only sampling of solar system material that is not processed in the peculiar manner of the earth was in meteorites. Meteorites therefore not only provide our best insight into the composition of the solar system, as discussed in Chapter 2, but also provide us with our best estimate of the age of the solar system.

All the methods for dating of long-time-scale events have been used effectively on meteorites. The results are shown in Table 7-2. It is clear that the age of the formation of meteorites and, by inference, the age of the planets is about 4.6 billion years. The oldest ages on lunar basalts obtained so far are about a half billion years younger than this, although the composite of material making up the lunar "soil"

Table 7-2   Dating Meteorites by Different Techniques (all showing maximum ages of 4.6 × 10⁹ years)

Dating Method	Types of Meteorites	Comments
Potassium-40/argon-40	Chondrites, achondrites, and silicates in irons	^{40}K decays by β^- decay 88% of the time to ^{40}Ca and by electron capture 12% to ^{40}Ar. $t_{1/2} = 1.3 \times 10^9$y. Some ages considerably lower due to ^{40}Ar loss
$(^{235}U + {}^{238}U + {}^{232}Th)/^4He$	Chondrites	Some ages considerably lower due to ^4He loss
Rubidium-87/ strontium-87	Chondrites, achondrites, and silicates in irons	Background daughter problem; to overcome use either several meteorites or separated minerals from a single meteorite to cover a range of rubidium to background strontium values. A plot of $^{87}Sr/Sr$ against Rb/Sr gives a line (*isochron*) whose slope yields the age and the intercept at $Rb/Sr = 0$ yields isotopic composition of background strontium. Commonly used half-life of 5.0×10^{10}y may be too high. Some lower ages because of secondary redistribution of nuclides
Uranium-lead	Irons and chondrites	Based on isochron made from several meteorites (see Fig. 7-3)

yields an age of about 4.6 billion years — not very different from the meteoritic ages, considering the present analytical uncertainties.

The Age of Crustal Events

We know that during the history of the earth many changes have taken place. Mountains have risen and been eroded, seas have covered the continents and retreated, deltas and other sediment configurations have been deposited and eroded or metamorphosed. Life has developed responding to the changing physical environment.

The record of these events has been preserved in rocks. The object of dating rocks by techniques based on radioactivity is to provide an "absolute" chronology, so that events can be correlated from continent to continent (and even under the oceans) and listed in proper sequence.

One important time point we seek is the age of the oldest rocks preserved on earth. Very old rocks indeed have been found by using each of the dating techniques. The age of the oldest rocks (which have been found in South Africa) is substantiated by two independent methods. One is the rubidium-strontium age. The second technique is to use lead deposits associated with these oldest rocks. The lead minerals, completely separated from uranium and thorium, act as recorders of the changing lead istope ratio as a function of time in a uranium-lead ratio reservoir which is changing only as the result of uranium decay (Fig. 7-3). These two techniques indicate that the oldest preserved rocks are about 3.5 billion years old. Since the age of the earth is 4.6 billion years this means that 1.1 billion years of the early history of the earth has been obscured by intensive reprocessing of the crust.

Granitic and metamorphic rocks from all over the world have been dated. It was stated in Chapter 5 that granitic and metamorphic rocks are clearly associated with

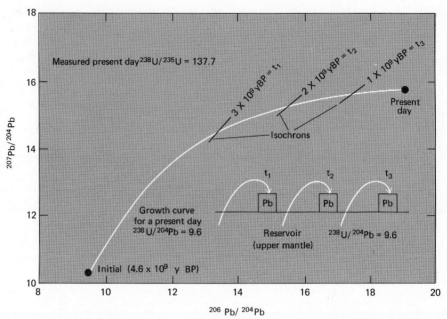

Figure 7-3 Dating of lead minerals. For a given $^{238}U/^{204}Pb$ ratio for a system a singular Pb isotope composition will result if a date and initial background Pb isotopic composition is assumed. Similarly for a common initial Pb isotope ratio, the Pb isotope ratios of samples developed in different $^{238}U/^{204}Pb$ ratio reservoirs will fall along a straight line at any given time passing through the initial Pb isotope ratio. This is called an *isochron* and its slope is directly related to age.

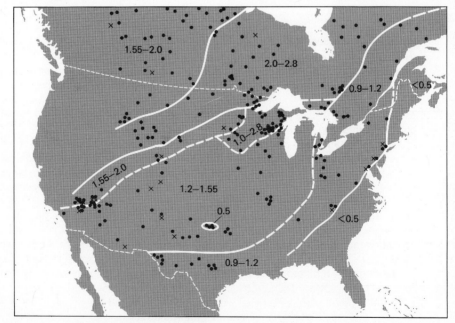

Figure 7-4 The distribution of ages of rocks (in billions of years) in the North American continent. From G. R. Tilton and S. R. Hart, *Science* **140,** 364 (1963). Copyright 1963 by the American Association for the Advancement of Science.

the building of mountains. Consequently, the implication is that by knowing the ages of formation of these rocks we are thereby dating ancient epochs of mountain building. Although old granitic and metamorphic terranes are overlaid in many places by younger sedimentary rock strata, a large number of dates have been obtained on these "basement" granitic and metamorphic rocks. From these dates it appears that each continent has a nucleus of very old rocks — 3 billion years or older. In North America the age distribution of granitic and metamorphic rocks resembles a zonal pattern, with the oldest rocks toward the interior and younger rocks progressively toward the edges of the continents (Fig. 7-4). The other continents do not show this apparent symmetrical structure but rather seem to be broken across the age boundaries.

In the study of the earth's crust the most important single concept has been that a time sequence can be based on the succession of fossil remains in rocks. Systems of rocks were described and defined from different parts of the world. Rocks of common age, as interpreted from the fact that they contain similar fossils, all over the world could be positioned relative to other systems of rocks. Since sequence in layered rocks is related to time, the ordering of the sedimentary rock systems relative to each other was also the ordering in time of events. From this, a geologic *time* scale was gradually developed (Fig. 7-5).

The rock systems were described independently by various geologists and provincial names were used to name them. The *Cambrian* system of rocks was described in Wales (the Roman name for Wales was *Cambria*); the *Ordovician* and *Silurian* systems of rocks were also described in Wales and were named after two ancient tribes that inhabited that region, the *Ordovices* and the *Silures*. The *Devonian* system was first described in the region of Devon in England; the *Mississippian,* along the bluffs of the Mississippi River; the *Pennsylvanian,* from the coal-bearing sequences of Pennsylvania; and the *Permian,* from the region of Perm in the U.S.S.R. Since the rocks of Cambrian through Permian systems appeared to be dominated by

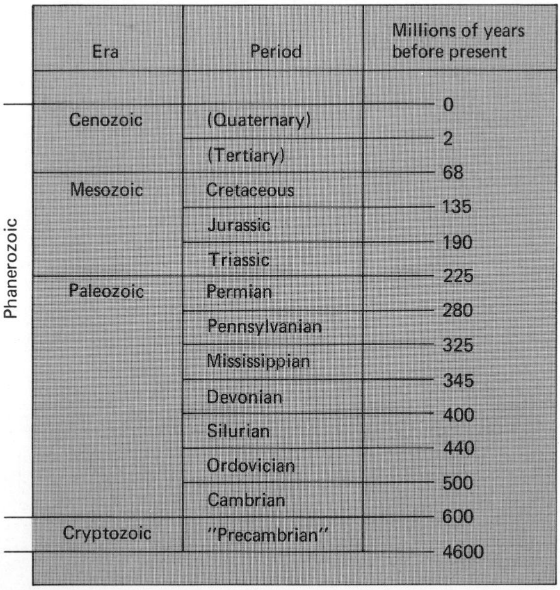

Era	Period	Millions of years before present
		0
Cenozoic	(Quaternary)	
		2
	(Tertiary)	
		68
Mesozoic	Cretaceous	
		135
	Jurassic	
		190
	Triassic	
		225
Paleozoic	Permian	
		280
	Pennsylvanian	
		325
	Mississippian	
		345
	Devonian	
		400
	Silurian	
		440
	Ordovician	
		500
	Cambrian	
		600
Cryptozoic	"Precambrian"	
		4600

(left vertical label: Phanerozoic)

Figure 7-5   The geologic time scale.

fossil remains of invertebrates, fishes, and amphibians, the time they represented was called the *Paleozoic ("old life") era* and the time represented by each *system* of rocks was called a *period.*

The terms *Triassic, Jurassic,* and *Cretaceous* are of continental European origin and together make up the so-called "age of reptiles." *Triassic* means "Threefold;" *Jurassic* is named after the Jura Mountains where the system of rocks was first described; and *Cretaceous* means "chalk," which was found to typify deposits of this age in Europe. (In the United States the Cretaceous is dominated by shales rather than limestones.) Together the three periods comprise the *Mesozoic ("middle life") era.*

The *Cenozoic ("recent life") era* is the most recent and is often called the "age of mammals." Although the Cenozoic era is still in its infancy on the geologic time scale (the Cenozoic *era* is also the Cenozoic *period*) it is subdivided into a sequence of *epochs* ranging from the oldest, *Paleocene,* to the most recent, *Pleistocene.*

The geologic time scale has been calibrated largely through dating of volcanic rocks found among some of the fossil-containing sedimentary rocks. Where the ideal "instantly deposited" volcanic rocks are lacking, one might try more indirect approaches such as dating granitic and metamorphic rocks lying *beneath* the sedimentary rock or those associated with a mountain-building event that also deformed already deposited sediments. Sediments that have never been deeply buried or deformed sometimes contain certain claylike minerals that can be dated by the potassium-argon or rubidium-strontium methods. The resulting chronology (Fig. 7-5) is now fairly well established.

Dating the Recent Past

Man is particularly sensitive to events of the recent past (say, the latest 5 million years) that have shaped his environment. Dating these events can give him a sense of perspective about the origins and migrations of his ancestors, and provide a base line for projecting what may happen in the near future. A number of techniques for dating the recent past are listed in Table 7-3.

Table 7-3 Techniques for Dating the Recent Past

Nuclide	Approximate Half-Life (years)	Range (years)	Applications
^{3}H	12	60	Glacial ice, wines
^{210}Pb	22	100	Glacial ice, lake deposits
^{226}Ra	1600	6000	Ocean circulation
^{32}Si	500	2000	Silceous deep-sea sediments
^{14}C	5500	35,000	Wood, charcoal, bones, shells, ocean circulation
^{10}Be	2.7×10^6	1×10^7	Deep-sea sediments
^{230}Th	7.5×10^4	3×10^5	Deep-sea sediments, corals,
^{234}U	2.5×10^5	5×10^5	travertines
^{231}Pa	3.2×10^4	1.5×10^5	

Reference

FAUL, H., *Ages of Rocks, Planets, and Stars.* New York: McGraw-Hill, 1966. 109 pp. Available in paperback.

8 The Evolution of the Earth

In the preceding chapters the materials of the earth have been described and the methods of determining the processes and time scales were explored. In this chapter an attempt will be made to look at the evolution of our planet. Since this is not a process that can be observed either in the laboratory or with the telescope, we commonly string together a sequence of reasonable arguments to arrive at a model or an approximation to reality as we see it at the moment. The discovery of some new piece of information about the earth, the solar system, or the galaxy may influence the chain of reasoning and hence the model. Despite the obvious fraility, then, of models of earth origins, the yearning to understand our earth in the context of its evolution drives us in the quest for a comprehensible plan.

Our questions are likely to be expressed in a number of different ways but they generally are resolvable into three major points: (1) the process of the formation of the solar system and the early history of the earth; (2) the origin of the ocean and atmosphere; and (3) the evolution of the earth's crust.

EARLY HISTORY OF THE EARTH AND SOLAR SYSTEM

When a star is being formed from a gas and dust cloud by gravitational collapse, it commonly inherits a rotational motion which will, if not accommodated, act to dissipate the protostar before it actually condenses. The star must transfer this rotational motion, or more accurately its *angular momentum,* to another part of the system (if we assume that it is at this stage a self-contained system), since the laws of mechanics require that in a closed system angular momentum must be conserved.

As the sphere of rotating gas contracts, the central portion becomes hotter because of the release of gravitational energy. At the same time a disk of gas, also heated up by the gravitational collapse, forms in a direction perpendicular to the axis of rotation (Fig. 8-1).

A star may lose angular momentum by forming a *binary star* system. The second star, formed from the flattened disk, rotates around the central protostar. Most of

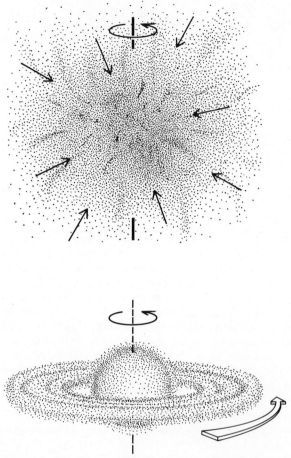

Figure 8-1 The formation of a disk of gas around a central rotating protosun. At the top the gravitational accretion results in a rotating mass which; as shown at the bottom, forms a central mass and a rotating disk.

the angular momentum of the system is then found in the rotation of the two stars around each other. Alternatively, the disk may become the site of small local condensations, finally to become planets (Fig. 8-1).

The evidence for this latter option is that our solar system actually exists! Although 99.85 percent of the mass of the solar system is in the sun, 95 percent of the angular momentum is in the orbiting planets, mainly Jupiter. Indeed, our solar system is a sort of binary star system in which Jupiter (which is not quite large enough to have lit up) and the sun are the two "stars."

To explain the details of the planet formation process a number of different models have been proposed (Table 8-1). To some degree they all call upon what has been learned from meteorites and, more recently, from the moon.

One model proposes that small *planetesimals,* originally made of metallic iron or silicate, were coalesced to form bodies resembling the ordinary chondrites. In the

Table 8-1   Three Possible Models for the Formation of the Solar System

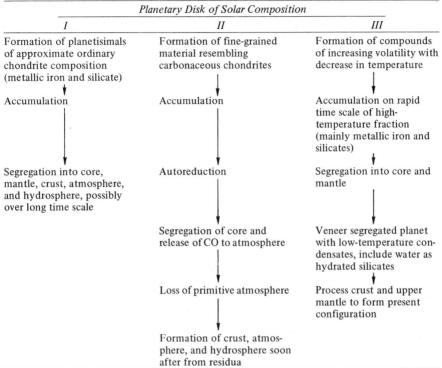

Planetary Disk of Solar Composition		
I	*II*	*III*
Formation of planetisimals of approximate ordinary chondrite composition (metallic iron and silicate)	Formation of fine-grained material resembling carbonaceous chondrites	Formation of compounds of increasing volatility with decrease in temperature
Accumulation	Accumulation	Accumulation on rapid time scale of high-temperature fraction (mainly metallic iron and silicates)
Segregation into core, mantle, crust, atmosphere, and hydrosphere, possibly over long time scale	Autoreduction	Segregation into core and mantle
	Segregation of core and release of CO to atmosphere	Veneer segregated planet with low-temperature condensates, include water as hydrated silicates
	Loss of primitive atmosphere	Process crust and upper mantle to form present configuration
	Formation of crust, atmosphere, and hydrosphere soon after from residua	

earth the metallic fraction segregated out to form the core, and subsequent degassing and selective melting of the whole earth produced the atmosphere, hydrosphere, and crust that we see today.

A second model suggests that carbonaceous chondrites represent the closest approximation to the raw material accumulating in the planets. Heating due to gravitational infall resulted in reactions similar to those in a blast furnace. Metallic iron-nickel formed by this process settled to the core and the silicate "slag" made up the remainder of the earth. A mass of carbon monoxide equaling about half the mass of the core was released to the surface of the planet, then removed from the atmosphere by an intense *solar wind* that streamed in during the sun's late stages of development. The residual surface material, after the loss of most of the primitive atmosphere, provided the ingredients of the present-day crust, atmosphere, and hydrosphere.

Both of these models call upon the accumulation of a relatively *homogenized* material from the primitive disk to form the planets. It is also possible to conceive of the accumulation of planetary material as a *heterogeneous* process.

The very existence of a planetary system obviously requires that the disk separate into several rings, which then condense independently. If the opacity of the condensing gas and dust is great enough, gravitationally produced heat is efficiently retained and the ring will heat up before it begins to cool off. At a pressure of about one thousandth of atmospheric pressure most of the material will be in a gaseous state at 2000°K. The least volatile compounds will condense first, followed by the condensation of more and more volatile compounds as cooling proceeds (Table 8-2). Calcium aluminum silicates are the first common materials to condense, followed by metallic iron-nickel and then magnesium silicates.

The accumulation of these highly refractory materials took place in less than 100,000 years, resulting in considerable heating up of the forming earth (perhaps as much as several thousand degrees centigrade). This, in turn, led to a complete separation of the earth into an iron-nickel core and a magnesium-iron silicate lower mantle. As the temperature dropped, finally the high volatility compounds – including metals like lead, mercury, thallium, and bismuth, the occluded rare gases, water in hydrated silicates (formed at low temperatures), and organic compounds – condensed, but on a slower time scale (perhaps over 10 million years). Any metallic iron left in the dust cloud would be converted first to iron sulfide and then to an iron oxide mineral, magnetite. These would also collect with the late-stage material on the primitive earth. The composition of this veneer of "volatile-rich" material is simulated by the carbonaceous chondrites.

The veneer material interacted with the surface of the planet where it was subjected to melting and magma formation. The shallower parts of the earth (upper mantle and crust) remain oxidized to this day because they have not come in contact with the iron-nickel core.

The moon is presumed to have accumulated adjacent to the earth. It missed the metallic iron portion by nucleating late in the condensation history. After capture by the earth very early in its history, it also missed the high volatility condensates that focused on the earth during their infall possibly because the center of mass of the earth-moon system is within the earth.

The oldest rocks on the earth date at about 3.5 billion years and they make up a sizable area of the earth's surface. The absence of older rocks seems to imply that

Table 8-2 The Equilibrium Condensation Sequence of Solid Phases from a Gas of Cosmic Composition and a Pressure of 10^{-3} Atmosphere[a]

Phase		Condensation Temperature (°K)	Temperature of Disappearance (°K)
Corundum	Al_2O_3	1758	1515
Perovskite	$CaTiO_3$	1647	1393
Melilite	$Ca_2Al_2SiO_7$	1625	1450
Spinel	$MgAl_2O_4$	1515	1362
Metallic iron	12.5 mole % Ni	1473	
Diopside	$CaMgSi_2O_6$	1450	
Forsterite	Mg_2SiO_4	1444	
	Ti_3O_5	1393	1125
Anorthite	$CaAl_2Si_2O_8$	1362	
Enstatite	$MgSiO_3$	1349	
Eskolaite	Cr_2O_3	1294	
Metallic cobalt	Co	1274	
Alabandite	MnS	1139	
Rutile	TiO_2	1125	
Alkali feldspar	$(Na,K)AlSi_3O_8$	$\sim$ 1050	
Troilite	FeS	700	
Magnetite	Fe_3O_4	405	
Ice	H_2O	$\leqslant$ 200	

[a] Modified from S. P. Clark, Jr., K. K. Turekian and L. Grossman in E. C. Robertson (Ed.), *The Nature of the Solid Earth*, McGraw-Hill (1972).

for the first billion years of earth history the reprocessing of the crust proceeded at a rapid rate. The processing would give the upper mantle and the crust its present-day distribution of elements.

HISTORY OF THE OCEAN AND ATMOSPHERE

However the earth accumulated, it evidently did not retain gases in any great quantity unless they were first trapped in solid material.

This fact becomes clear when we compare the abundances of the rare gases in the atmosphere relative to the silicon content of the earth (as the most convenient solid-forming element for normalization) against the same ratio estimated for the primitive gas from which the solar system was formed (Fig. 8-2). The earth's quota of the rare gases was evidently depleted by factors of billions compared with their primitive abundances. It follows that the atmosphere and the hydrosphere of the earth had to be derived from the earth by degassing of the accumulated solid material, and not as a residue of an original atmosphere.

The normal processes of weathering of crystalline silicate rocks fall short of providing the carbon dioxide, water, and nitrogen of the oceans and atmosphere. In fact, weathering products and sediments actually tend to use up carbon dioxide (to convert a silicate rock to limestone, for example) and water (to convert anhydrous minerals to hydrated clays). The elements that are found in the hydrosphere and

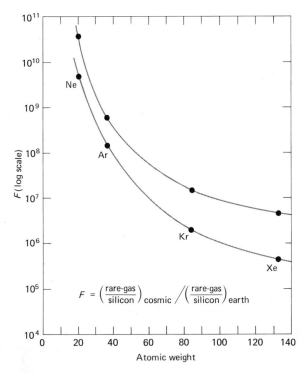

$$F = \left(\frac{\text{rare-gas}}{\text{silicon}}\right)_{\text{cosmic}} \bigg/ \left(\frac{\text{rare-gas}}{\text{silicon}}\right)_{\text{earth}}$$

Figure 8-2 The fractionation of the rare gases with respect to silicon in the earth relative to the primitive solar nebula. After H. Brown in G. P. Kuiper (Ed.), *The Atmospheres of the Earth and Planets*, University of Chicago Press (1952).

atmosphere that cannot be derived by weathering of igneous rocks have been called *excess volatiles* (Table 8-3).

The question remains as to whether the earth degassed massively in its early history or whether the atmosphere and hydrosphere have been slowly and continuously supplied over the history of the earth. Volcanoes, fumaroles, geysers, and hot springs indicate that water vapor and other gases are coming to the surface of the earth, but other evidence points to a major recycling rather than a brand-new appearance of the water and other gases. For instance, it has been shown that whenever rain containing radioactive tritium from nuclear bomb detonation falls on a geyser terrane, the geyser water shows the pulse of tritium soon afterward. Other evidence for large-scale cycling of the upper mantle and crust is discussed in the next section. Hence, despite the fact that material may be supplied from the depths of the earth, the rate of emergence at the surface is too slow to be detected in the presence of a "background" of crustal and upper-mantle recycling.

The presence of an early ocean and atmosphere is inferred from the types of the earliest rocks found, but as we have seen, even the oldest rocks date more than one billion years younger than the age of the earth. During that "lost interval" all the volatiles of the earth could have been derived and recycled many times, while the evidence for the exact mechanism of supply was obliterated completely.

At present there are two lines of argument favoring a rapid appearance (within the first billion years) of the atmosphere and oceans.

1. The presence of shallow seas on the continents more or less continuously since about 3 billion years ago, requiring a deep ocean over the rest of the earth to act as the ultimate reservoir.

2. Evidence from the study of the atmosphere of Venus that the present-day loss rate of water from that planet's atmosphere (which equals the rate of degassing of its interior) is extremely small. Since Venus had earlier lost its surficial water (evidenced by the large amount of CO_2 found in the atmosphere) there is no recycling of water back into the mantle of Venus as there is on earth. The degassing rate for Venus applied to its "twin sister," earth, indicates that only one millionth of the oceans could have been supplied at this rate to the earth's surface over 4.6 billion years.

Even if we accept the early formation of the ocean and atmosphere, their compositions at each point of time in the earth's history are problematical. If ascending water "flushed" the primitive rocks, the sodium chloride in the oceans could be accounted for, implying that the early established saltiness of the oceans remained about the

Table 8-3 The "Excess" Volatiles: Compounds at the Earth's Surface Not Available from the Weathering of Igneous Rocks[a]

Compound	Amount on Earth's Surface Not Derived by Weathering ($\times 10^{20}$ grams)
Water	16,600
Total carbon as carbon dioxide	910
Chlorine	300
Nitrogen	42
Sulfur	22

[a] After W. W. Rubey. Geological Society of America, Special Paper 62 (1955)

same ever since. However, since there are no similar constraints for the sulfate, bicarbonate, or the cation concentrations of the ocean, these could vary with time to some degree, and probably did.

The question of whether the oxygen level in the atmosphere could have been as high in the past is an open one. Oxygen can be produced by decomposition of water molecules in air by the action of ultraviolet radiation on water molecules in the atmosphere, with subsequent escape of hydrogen into space. Some calculations indicate that this process can be remarkably efficient, so the oxygen level throughout most of earth history could have been as high as at present. Other researchers believe that without biological photosynthesis the oxygen level would be maintained only at a fairly low level. (For an oxygen-rich atmosphere there will be a tendency for nitrate to be formed and dissolve in the sea. At present this tendency is balanced by the return of nitrogen to the atmosphere through biological processes. When such processes became active the nitrogen level was maintained in the atmosphere.)

Unfortunately the evidence from ancient rocks is ambiguous regarding the history of oxygen in the atmosphere. The presence of easily oxidizable compounds in ancient stream-transported deposits indicates to some people that the atmosphere was almost anoxic 3 billion years go, whereas others see these deposits as being made by special processes of deposition in anoxic bottoms of estuaries, lakes, and streams where protection from dissolution is inhibited, during transportation, by organic coatings. Both groups are able to find modern analogs that support their positions.

THE EVOLUTION OF THE CRUST OF THE EARTH

The record in the rocks becomes more and more complete the nearer we approach the present. Many rocks now exposed on the continents were deposited in vast seas, and contain a clearly recognizable spectrum of fossilized marine organisms that were present at least 600 million years ago and probably for many millions of years before that.

In light of this fact, a dilemma arises when we look at the ocean bottom. This enormous area, occupying 71 percent of the earth's surface, and covered by 4000 meters of protective seawater, should retain as complete a record of the earth's history as we find anywhere on land, if not more so. Yet, no sediments older than about 150 million years have been recovered from the ocean bottom, nor do we expect to recover anything older on the basis of measured sediment thicknesses and rates of sediment accumulation. It is as if, in the ocean, we are looking at a continually renewed part of the earth that has a transitory memory of only 150 million years, whereas the continents remember events 25 times older.

If we accept a view that the *ocean bottoms* are continuously renovated by cycling of some sort, this view is seen to be only an extension of the gradual realization that much of what is in the *ocean basins* has also been recycled. Hence, in the broadest terms we may have to view the oceans as a *steady-state* system in which things go in and things go out but the net properties of the system are not grossly altered.

Water Cycles Between Land and Sea

The writer of the Book of Ecclesiastes was aware of one aspect of the cycles of the sea when he wrote: "The rivers run into the sea and the sea is not full." And of

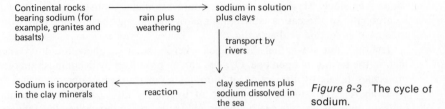

Figure 8-3   The cycle of sodium.

course the reason for this is that evaporation from the sea and subsequent rainfall on land is the source of the rivers that run back into the sea. In Chapter 6 we saw that the mean residence time of water in the oceans is 40,000 years. (This means that in the length of time equivalent to the *mean residence time,* 63 percent of the original molecules of water in the ocean identified at the beginning of this interval will have been cycled. And after three mean residence times have elapsed, 95 percent of the original water molecules will have undergone the recycling experience.)

The Cycles of Stream-Transported Materials

John Joly in 1901 reasoned that, if one measures the amount of sodium in the sea, one should be able to get an age of the ocean (and by inference, the age of the earth). Sodium is not capable of forming a vapor at surface temperatures; thus we

Figure 8-4   The White Cliffs of Dover (Shakespeare Cliff) made of coccolith chalk. With permission of the British Travel Association.

might expect that once it is transported somewhere it should stay there. If the average sodium concentration of streams is 6.3 parts per million and in seawater it is 10,760 parts per million, then, knowing the volume of the ocean and rate of river flow, we can calculate, on a unidirectional model, the length of time required to supply the ocean's stock of sodium. This age turns out to be 68 million years. Since we know that seawater of approximately present-day volume and salinity must have existed long before that time (as inferred from the types and distribution of fossils), this "age" clearly is not a true age but is to be interpreted as a *mean residence time* of sodium in the sea, in the same way that it is considered to be for water.

But if sodium is not lost by evaporation, what are the mechanisms of its removal? Some of it is transferred back to the continents by forming aerosols, which act as the nuclei for raindrops. Some may be trapped in interspaces in the loose sediment deposited on the ocean floor. But most of it must react with clay on the ocean bottom. The ultimate source of these clay minerals is the weathering of continental rocks, which is also the source of the sodium not otherwise accounted for by the supply by rain. Our view of the cycle of sodium through the ocean is shown in Fig. 8-3. Clearly this is a cycle only in the sense that we have managed to find a device for keeping the oceans in a steady-state concentration level of sodium. We have ignored the possibility that the ocean-bottom deposits may get transferred back to the continents, to complete the cycle in reality.

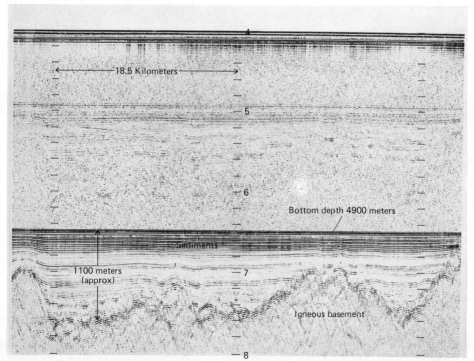

Figure 8-5 A seismic reflection profile of an abyssal plain, showing the burying of topography by detrital sediments. (9°30′ N 44°35′ W). Courtesy of Teledyne Exploration Company.

Figure 8-6 A representation of the topography of the ocean basins in the Atlantic Ocean showing the major ocean ridge system. From B. C. Heezen, M. Tharp, and M. Ewing, The Geological Society of America, Special Paper 65 (1959).

Indeed, as long as we omit this last part of the cycle, we can solve many marine cycle problems. In this myopic, but commonly useful, view we can distribute the materials taken to the ocean into a variety of sedimentary reservoirs in the ocean basins, without any anguish about their ultimate fate.

We become uneasy, however, when we begin to project the process into the future, because there is obviously only a limited amount of material. This is most clearly seen in the case of calcium, the major constituent of bones and shells. Most of the calcium carried in solution by rivers is derived from the weathering of limestone, which, after being dissolved and taken to the sea, is deposited as calcium carbonate primarily by single-celled organisms of the deep sea in the form of coccoliths (the major component of the White Cliffs of Dover, Fig. 8-4) and foraminiferan shells. The amount of calcium carbonate deposited as clamshells and coral reefs

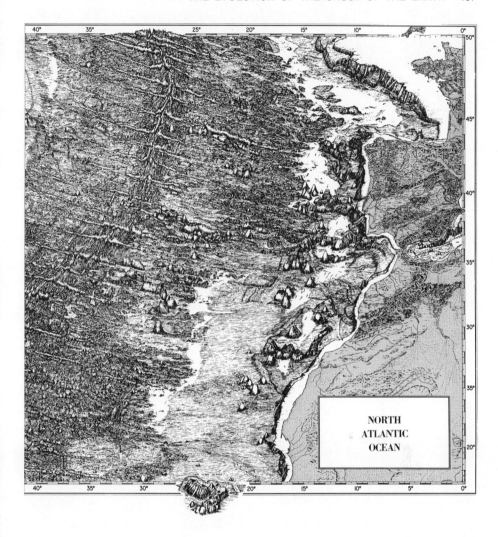

NORTH
ATLANTIC
OCEAN

is trivial by comparison. If we follow this ravaging of the continents by weathering and transportation of the calcium to the sea and watch its deposition in the deep ocean for as long as the "stockpile" of limestone on the continents remains, we discover that the continents will be stripped of limestone in 100 million years and the calcium carbonate derived from it, all deposited along the apparently inaccessible major oceanic ridge systems of the world, such as the mid-Atlantic ridge or the East Pacific rise.

This situation is intolerable; somehow we must believe that there is a recycling process for calcium carbonate. Recycling can happen either by redissolving some of the calcium carbonate deposited in the deep sea and transporting and depositing it in shallow environments adjacent to the continents, or by the physical transfer of the ocean bottom sediments to the continents.

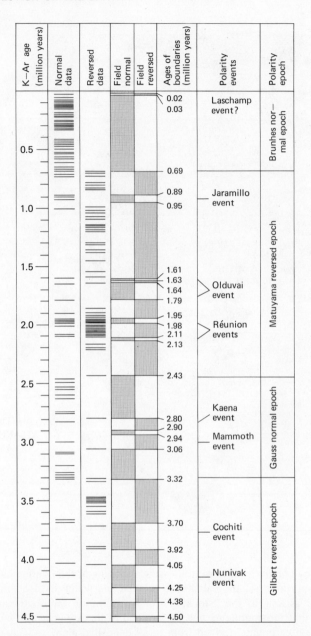

Figure 8-7 The changes in magnetic polarity of the earth as recorded in lava flows. From A. Cox, *Science,* **163,** 237 (1969). Copyright 1969 by the American Association for the Advancement of Science.

Using the two examples of sodium and calcium, we can satisfy most of their cycles in a simple way for time scales that are short. Our sense of triumph at discovering oceanic depositories is overshadowed by the fact that cycle stories must all come to an end on a very short time scale—a fate not permitted by our reading of the geologic record and our projection of it into the future. We are then forced to look for a way out by a return of these elements to the continents.

Perhaps the clearest example of this compelling pressure to recycle the *whole* surface of the earth, including the ocean and its deposits, comes from the study of the supply and disposition of the solids (the *detrital* load) carried by streams. Whereas the average concentration of dissolved material (sodium, calcium, and so on) is 120 parts per million, the worldwide detrital load is 400 parts per million.

The detritus and much of the dissolved load comes from the weathering and erosion of continental rocks: granites, basalts, metamorphic rocks, and sedimentary rocks. The continuous transport of detritus to the ocean results in the gradual denudation of the continents. Indeed, if the "eternal" mountains were not continually uplifted, at the present rates of denudation the continents would all be at sea level in 10 to 20 million years. On the other side of the argument, if the detritus from the continents keeps piling up in the ocean basins without any subsequent action (Fig. 8-5), in about 70 million years the whole ocean will be "silted up" (to use a term normally applied to basins behind dams).

If the processes we see operating today operated in the past, then we must (1) get material to the continents from somewhere to keep the land high, and (2) get rid of the accumulating debris in the oceans. Luckily, just such a convenient set of operations is available in the new models of ocean-basin history derived from geophysical observations.

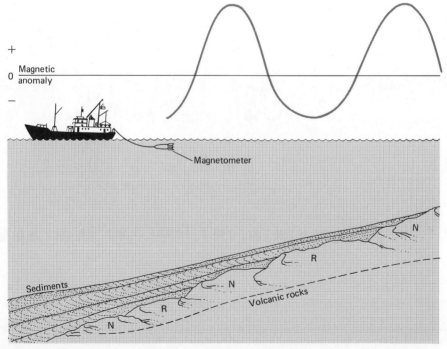

Figure 8-8 An idealized diagram showing the effect of submarine lava flow magnetic polarity orientation on the magnetic pattern observed with a magnetometer towed by a ship.

The Surface of the Earth in Motion

There are three major geophysical observations that provide the basis for viewing the ocean basins in cyclical terms: (1) the distribution of the major oceanic ridge systems with their associated volcanic activity and the distribution of deep trenches; (2) polarity reversals of the earth's magnetic field; and (3) the distribution of "deep-focus" earthquakes.

The major oceanic ridge systems form a series of connected, topographically high areas present in all the oceans. Ridges are between 1000 and 4000 km wide, with a relief of 2 to 4 km above the ocean floor, protruding here and there as islands (Fig. 8-6). The term "mid-oceanic ridge" has sometimes been used for the system, after the most prominent example, the mid-Atlantic ridge. The topography is representative of a composite of volcanic and rupture features called *faults*. At the center of the mid-Atlantic ridge, for example, there is a discontinuous rift valley, characterized by heavy but entirely shallow-focus earthquake activity and higher-than-average heat flow. A series of transverse trenches that offset the axis of the ridge is also prominent. Other oceanic ridges, such as the East Pacific rise, have many of the elements of the mid-Atlantic ridge, but not necessarily all. Nevertheless, these differences aside, the ridges appear to be continuous around the earth, except for offsetting by transverse breaks. They are a major feature of the ocean basins, coupled in some way to the location of continents.

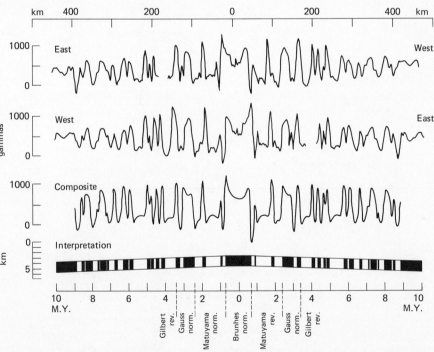

Figure 8-9 The symmetrical magnetic anomalies around the axis of the mid-ocean ridge systems (here shown for the East Pacific Rise 50°S 120°W) From W. C. Pitman and J. R. Heirtzler, *Science,* **154,** 1164 (1966). Copyright 1966 by the American Association for the Advancement of Science.

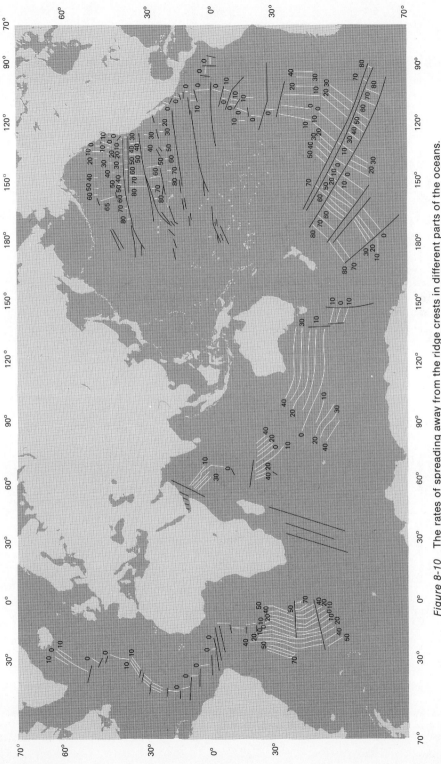

Figure 8-10 The rates of spreading away from the ridge crests in different parts of the oceans. J. R. Heirtzler, *et al., Journal of Geophysical Research* **73**, 2119 (1968).

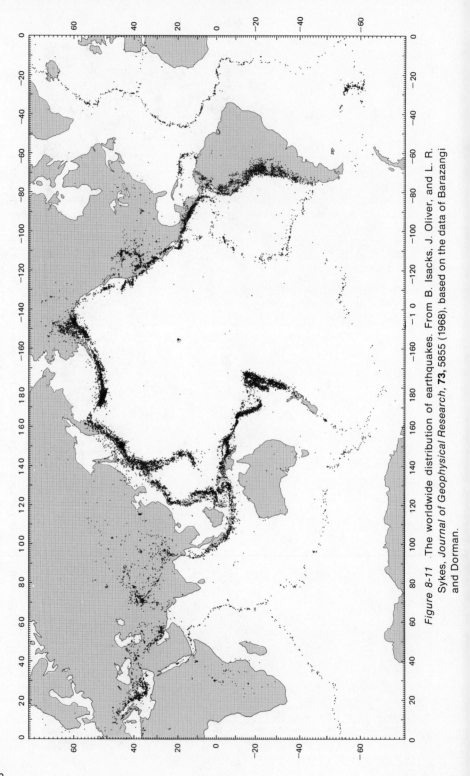

Figure 8-11 The worldwide distribution of earthquakes. From B. Isacks, J. Oliver, and L. R. Sykes, *Journal of Geophysical Research*, **73**, 5855 (1968), based on the data of Barazangi and Dorman.

In many parts of the world, the continental margin beyond the shelf plunges off into a deep trench. These trenches, especially prominent around the Pacific ocean basin, are the deepest parts of the ocean, often exceeding 9 km in depth.

The major oceanic ridge systems are also sites of volcanic activity. We know that when a lava flow begins to crystallize, the magnetic minerals respond to the magnetic polarity existing at the time of extrusion. The magnetization is sufficiently strong to survive the vicissitudes of geologic time, provided the temperature is not raised too high or major chemical alteration does not take place. Lava flows, then, act as a record of the changing magnetic polarity of the earth (Fig. 8-7). Although carefully oriented volcanic rock samples on land have been used to document the changing polarity of the past 4 million years, such an approach is not possible for submarine volcanic material. Dredging volcanic rock samples from the bottom of the sea gives no information on orientation.

A sensitive *magnetometer* (an instrument that measures the earth's magnetic intensity), towed by a ship or airplane, is able to sense the small local variations in magnetic intensity. If rocks containing magnetic material have formed in the earth's present-day polarity, they reinforce the magnetic effect measured by the magnetometer, whereas if the polarity had been reversed at the time of the solidification of the lava, the present-day magnetic intensity would be diminished by the reversely

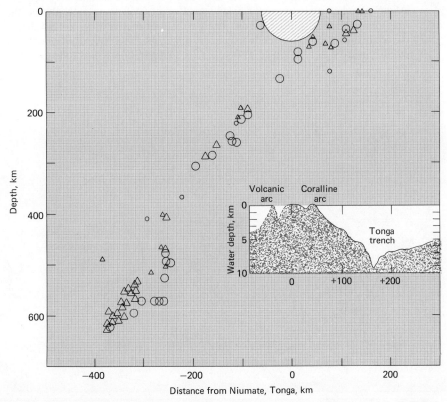

Figure 8-12 The earthquake foci along trenches. From B. Isacks, J. Oliver, and L. R. Sykes, *Journal of Geophysical Research*, **73**, 5855 (1968).

magnetized rocks (Fig. 8-8). Either of these effects results in so-called *magnetic anomalies.*

Surveys of the major oceanic ridge systems have revealed symmetrical magnetic-anomaly patterns about the crests of the ridges (Fig. 8-9). The pattern implies that if the major volcanic activity has been happening at the crest, resulting in the emplacement of basaltic lavas magnetized in the field orientation at the time of extrusion, then the ridges must be pulling apart to allow the recording of new events by ever younger submarine lava flows. The magnetic-anomaly patterns can be related directly to the sequence of known magnetic reversals determined from oriented volcanic rocks on land. The horizontal distance between the crest and so-dated magnetic boundaries yields the rate of spreading of the ocean floor for a particular part of the ridge system (Fig. 8-10). For example, the rate for the southern mid-Atlantic ridge is 1 cm/yr, whereas it is 4.5 cm/yr for the southern East Pacific rise. This observation is the clearest single evidence for the fact that the ocean floors are highly mobile and, indeed, spreading away from the ridges.

The distribution of earthquakes geographically and with depth has been cataloged now for many years, and clear patterns emerge (Fig. 8-11). The major oceanic ridge areas are demarked by more earthquakes than the rest of the ocean basin, except for the oceanic margins, with which deep trenches are associated. The earthquakes along the ridges have shallow foci (less than 100 km and commonly less than 50 km). Along trenches and associated island arcs or coastal mountains, the earthquakes are both shallow and deep focus. The earthquake foci in these areas fall along 45-degree planes, dipping under the island arcs or coastal mountains, ultimately reaching depths as great as 800 km (Fig. 8-12). This configuration seems to imply movement

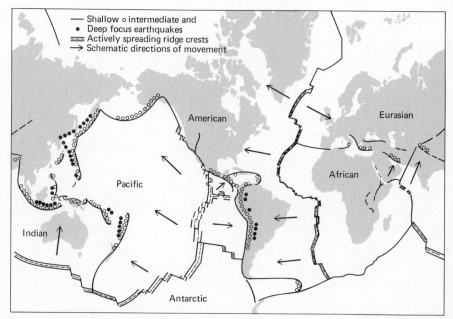

Figure 8-13   A diagrammatic representation of the moving plate making up the earth's surface. From F. Vine, *Journal of Geological Education,* **17,** 6 (1969).

along the plane and is interpreted to mean that oceanic sheets are compressed against, and plunge under, either sheets with a more continental aspect or adjacent oceanic sheets.

Combining these three sets of observations, the following picture can be drawn of the nature of the ocean bottom.

One can imagine the earth's surface to be made of about seven (or more) plates, each of which is bounded by two or more of the other plates either by a line of rupture at which the plates are separating (the major oceanic ridges) or by a line of compression, in which one plate is pushed under the other plate (trenches) (Fig. 8-13). The part of the plate that is pushed under is mainly oceanic material, not continental. The thickness of the plates (or, as some have decided to call the assemblage of plates, the *lithosphere*) is about 150 km, which is considerably greater than the thickness assigned to the conventional *crust* (11 to 40 km) (Fig. 8-14). At the base of the 150 km plate is a region of weakness (the *asthenosphere*) which accommodates this movement. This depth was chosen mainly because it also corresponds to a region of exceptionally low velocity for seismic waves and may have a small amount of melted material, acts as a "lubricant."

Hence the cycles of the sea, which to the ancient philosophers dealt simply with the transport of water (the most obvious component of the ocean), now are known to involve the dissolved salts, the suspended detritus, and, ultimately, the whole ocean bottom itself. The present-day scientists present us with an ocean that may be as old as the earth itself but, because of the inexorable properties of the earth's interior, is perpetually renewed.

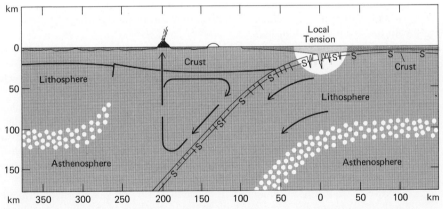

Figure 8-14 The relationship between the structure and seismic properties of the crust and upper mantle and the interpretation of the subduction zone where two plates collide. From B. Isacks, J. Oliver, and L. R. Sykes, *Journal of Geophysical Research,* **73,** 5855 (1968).

References

ROBERTSON, E. C. (ed.), *The Nature of the Solid Earth.* New York: McGraw-Hill, 1972, 677 pp.

TAKEUCHI, H., S. UYEDA, and H. KANAMORI, *Debate about the Earth.* San Francisco, Calif.: Freeman, Cooper & Co., 1970, 281 pp. (revised ed.). Available in paperback.

9 Epilogue: Man Interacts with His Environment

All life influences the environment and in turn is influenced by it. Beaver dams inundate small patches of forest, killing the trees. Plant life and bacteria transform rocks into soil, permitting them to crumble under the action of the weather. The "red tide" in the oceans in areas of high-nutrient element supply causes mass mortality among fish by creating an excess of chemicals toxic to the fish. But these are all parts of nature and, although destructive, they form a pattern that can be reconciled with the ongoing cycle of life.

Man has mimicked much that plants and animals can do, but under his assault the cycle of nature is broken and a man-controlled earth is in the offing. We have gone beyond the ancient charge to "subdue the earth" and in many ways are clearly ravaging it. This is the crisis of man interacting with his environment!

There was at one time the fear that man would use up the natural resources that earth supplied, but this fear has gradually been assuaged as we developed confidence in the optimistic results of exploration, exploitation, and substitution. However, the more immediate problem is what we appear to be doing by the creation of virtually indestructible wastes, highly toxic wastes, and chemicals of doubtful benignity when widely used.

Nevertheless, a polemic approach to the problem of man and the environment is hardly a substitute for a careful look at the technological and social problems. We have come to take unlimited electric power, airplanes, and motorcycles, and an efficient communication system for granted and tend to forget that *somewhere,* on some scale, large or small, land is being scarred to mine metals to make electronic equipment and machines, toxic chemicals are dumped into streams as the result of paper manufacture, and waters in confined bays are being used for cooling of power plants. A high level of integrity requires that we consider the role of every man in exacerbating the problem. To do this properly we must understand the major efforts of man and how they affect his management of the environment. First we shall consider the mineral and chemical resources of the earth; then we shall explore the effect of the size and needs of an evergrowing population on the environment.

MINERAL RESOURCES

Undoubtedly, among the first mineral resources that man used were rocks, which at first were simply hurled in self-defense, but ultimately were employed in more sophisticated ways for making tools. Rocks were used as early as about 10,000 years ago for building houses and walls – an application that has been complemented but not replaced in many parts of the world today.

The use of mud for pots and bricks followed quickly behind the use of rocks. Sun-dried bricks and pots were utilized extensively into the peak of Mesopotamian civilization about 5000 years ago, when the discovery was made that permanent strength is greatly increased by kilning.

Concurrently with the development of materials for the basic needs (shelter, defense, hunting, and agriculture), the esthetic appreciation of different kinds of rocks and minerals grew.

Sometime during this age of primitive exploration, native (metallic) gold, silver, copper, and possibly iron (as meteoritic iron) were discovered, and their properties of ductility, malleability, and luster were exploited for ornamental and (especially copper) for practical use.

The hot fires of the kilning ovens led to conscious and unconscious experimentation. Tin was extracted as the metal from its oxide ore as early as 4000 years ago in ancient Troy. The discovery of a number of metals with different properties undoubtedly led to experimentation in alloying, the first result being the useful alloy of tin and copper called bronze. This alloy was harder than either of its pure components, allowing the improvement of weapons and agricultural tools.

But not until about 3000 years ago, when widespread smelting of iron ore began, was there a major breakthrough in the general use of metals. New metals and alloys of these metals found a place in the fabric of cultures throughout the world, though not always on the same time scale. From this brief historical picture we see that a *resource* is recognized only as man discovers it and learns to exploit it. If no one considered gold to be valuable it would not be considered a resource.

On a more technical level, any concentration of a desired element or compound can be called an *ore deposit*. In addition, some undesired material (*gangue*) usually must be processed. Smelting or refining processes may discriminate further against elements that were not sought after at the time. For instance, during the work of the Curies on radium, huge quantities of uranium ore were processed; radium was extracted and the uranium was discharged. A generation later the *uranium* became the sought after element and the discharge piles were processed again – this time for uranium.

Ore deposits are concentrations of an element or other mineral material that are economically exploitable at the moment of search. They may be rich, high-grade deposits or low-grade, but often very large, deposits. During a time of low demand and large abundance of easily discoverable high-grade deposits, low-grade deposits may be ignored or even overlooked during exploration. As the demand grows and the number of high-grade deposits diminishes, ever-lower-grade deposits become economically interesting. Possibly all desired elements can be found and extracted at about any level of concentration if enough energy were available. With the advent of nuclear energy and, in particular, the prospect of controlled fusion reactions becoming more and more realistic, the energy resource will be unlimited. It would seem, at least superficially, that if we want any element badly enough, sufficient energy will some day be available to extract it from even the lowest grade ore deposits.

Although this fact seems clear it also provides a warning that the patterns we have come to expect in the continued technological improvement of the world may be in jeopardy if the costs of extraction of desirable resources from the earth increase. Up to now we have depended on the increasing efficiency of mining and extraction of metals to match the ever-lower-grade ore that must be mined. But there is evidence that a plateau in cost may have been reached, and that cost of metals in the future will gradually increase if the projected demands are sustained. An alternative to processing ever-lower-grade ores is to look to reprocessing desirable metals from scrap and waste. We already do this on a large scale with scrap iron. Other metals may also be recoverable in such a fashion.

POLLUTION

As we already noted, many acts of living creatures are threats to the existence of some other creatures. The wealth of ecological diversity, however, has prevented the complete deterioration of life on earth. But man now threatens by his acts to make the habitat a highly man-oriented environment. Hopefully the vastness of nature and man's deep-seated curatorial sense will act together to prevent such an irreversible change.

Man, however, has the capacity to be harsher with his own species than any other. Wars and pogroms through the ages clearly attest to this. It is not an exaggeration that man can today destroy himself almost instantly with nuclear, chemical, or biological weapons.

If, in our optimism, we think that a policy of military deterrence will prevent such a final act, we soon discover that man's self-destructive potentials are not restricted to catastrophic events but can operate on much longer time scales. Curiously, we are tolerating the slow conversion of a pure atmosphere to one that can cause or aggravate respiratory illnesses, and are permitting the casual conversion of pure waterways into dumping grounds for sewage, chemicals, and refuse with concurrent health and comfort deterioration for mankind.

How can we meet the present challenges posed by these acts of destruction? We can attempt to solve the problems technologically and scientifically; that is, we can look for ways of managing our terrestrial housekeeping to minimize the fouling of our environment. To a large degree it can be safely assumed that if technology or science were the only problem standing in the way we could keep our environment relatively pure. All that we would require is an unlimited source of energy!

However, even if money were not the limiting factor in obtaining energy, we would run into another problem. The use of energy means that fuels and coolant devices are required. The end result for any useful energy-producing system is thermal pollution. Waterways and the air in local environments would be the dumping grounds for this heat. The result is not easily predictable, but it is likely that the ecology of the environment will be modified. At our present rate of use of fossil and nuclear fuels we can project that by the year 2000 the generation of heat at the surface of the earth by man's machines will be equivalent to 2 percent of the sun's heat reaching the earth, and this proportion could continue to increase until sometime in the near future the rate of man-initiated heat production approaches, or possibly exceeds, the heat from the sun available to the earth. To counteract this undesirable effect there are the "ice buffers" at the poles. When all the glacial ice on Antarctica and Greenland melts, the sea level will rise 60 meters and most of our major maritime cities will be jeopardized by flooding! After that, the temperature of the earth's surface will increase and more water vapor from the oceans can be expected to be stored in the atmosphere. The additional vapor would act as a heat blanket in the troposphere, making the surface of the earth warmer still. Although this may make the newly exposed land in the high latitudes, formerly covered by glaciers, more livable, it will undoubtedly bring discomfort to the middle and lower latitudes. All in all it would require a new way of life.

Let us suppose that such a state will not come about or that the concern for the immediate future overshadows that for long-term effects. Let us assume that the scientific and technological tools exist for a clean environment *now*. These tools will not be used for alleviating the pollution problems unless strong social and economic pressures are applied against offending organizations. New pollution-attenuating devices and programs will mean an increased cost to the country (or the world) if we continue to operate at a high level of industrialization. The immediate consequences of this are not clear. It may mean a retarded rate of production, with continued hardships for the poor and unemployed.

All of these predictions are based on an evergrowing population, becoming ever more sophisticated in its demands for goods and services. If the population growth rate can be slowed or actually brought to zero, our chances are that much more improved to persist without major dislocations or discomforts. Only mankind as a whole can ultimately decide these questions. Small-scale frugalities will not solve the problem.

References

CLOUD, P. E., *Resources and Man*. San Francisco, Calif.: W. H. Freeman and Co., 1969, 259 pp. Available in paperback.

SKINNER, B. J., *Earth Resources*. Englewood Cliffs, N.J.: Prentice-Hall, 1969, 149 pp. Available in paperback.

Committee on Chemistry and Public Affairs. "Cleaning Our Environment: The Chemical Basis for Action." *A Report by the Subcommittee on Environmental Improvement*. Washington, D.C.: American Chemical Society, 1969, 249 pp. Available in paperback.

Appendix I
Chemical Equilibrium and Phase Diagrams

The concept of equlibrium implies a state of no action or balanced action. A ball rolls from the top of a hill into the valley and stops; a piece of ice on a hot summer day melts and the resulting puddle of water takes on the ambient (surrounding) temperature; an empty bottle thrown into the ocean fills with water and sinks; a log turns to ashes in a fireplace – all these are examples of physical or chemical systems that move toward equilibrium. That is, movement or change spontaneously proceeds from a *less* stable to a *more* stable situation. The most stable situation is called the *equilibrium* state.

In all the preceding examples we may define a quantity that is always minimized or maximized during the approach to equilibrium. The rolling ball loses *potential energy* (converting it to kinetic energy); the burning log gives off *heat;* and so forth. In chemical reactions a similar optimization of a property of the system is followed as an indicator of the trend toward equilibrium. This property is called *free energy*. In a spontaneous reaction *free energy* decreases as the chemical reaction proceeds toward equilibrium.

Suppose that we go to an unusually well-equipped chemical storeroom shelf and choose metallic sodium, metallic aluminum, and metallic silicon. If we mix these (carefully isolating them from oxygen and water until we are ready) in the proportion of one mole of sodium, one mole of aluminum, and three moles of silicon we will have the same ratio of these elements as in albite ($NaAlSi_3O_8$). All we need to add is oxygen. Let us raise the temperature of our oxygen- and water-free charge to about 600°C to accelerate the reaction and then open the system to oxygen.

The reaction will proceed, releasing a large definite amount of energy, in the following way:

$$Na + Al + 3Si + 4O_2 \rightarrow NaAlSi_3O_8$$

Clearly, the stable material at 600°C in the presence of oxygen is albite and not the starting mixture. The free energy of the system has decreased and albite is the material that is in equilibrium with air at 600°C.

Of course, rocks are not made this way in nature. Igneous rock, for instance, crystallizes from magma in which oxygen is already present. At a given temperature and composition, a particular assemblage of minerals of specific compositions will form.

Let us consider first a magma composed of the proportions: one atom of Fe^{+2}, one atom of Mg^{+2}, one atom of Si^{+4}, and four atoms of O^{-2}. You will recognize this as equivalent to olivine with the composition $MgFeSiO_4$. In the laboratory, let us melt such a mixture, then gradually cool it (Fig. A-1). As we do so, the first crystal that forms is olivine with the formula $Mg_{1.8}Fe_{0.2}SiO_4$. Our artificial magma becomes depleted in magnesium relative to iron to balance this. As the temperature drops the crystals that are forming by reaction with the melt will have a unique composition at each temperature as will its associated melt, as determined by Fig. A-1. This is called a *phase diagram* of a *binary system with solid solution.* (When all the liquid has crystallized, the crystal will have the exact composition of the original melt. Clearly, if any crystals are removed from the system as the temperature drops, the last crystals formed would be decidedly higher in iron than the original melt.) A *phase* is any part of a system that has either a homogeneous chemical composition, or one that varies continuously and predictably to its boundary, through which it is clearly separated from another phase. The system we are considering has two phases — liquid and olivine crystals.

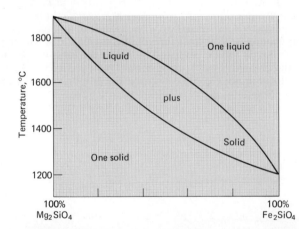

Figure A-1   Phase diagram for olivine.

We can define the number of chemical *components* in a system as the minimum number of chemical species, hypothetical or real, that can be used to describe the system. Since we can describe the olivine phase diagram by assuming a solid solution between pure Fe_2SiO_4 and pure Mg_2SiO_4, the number of components is *two.*

In addition, there are two other common variables in natural systems: temperature and pressure.

How can we describe the system if one or more of these quantities is known? It so happens that if the number of phases equals the number of variables (number of components plus temperature and pressure), then the composition of phase and the temperature and pressure are specified. We say that the system is "completely determined." If the number of variables *exceeds* the number of phases, an uncertainty exists and further independent information must be specified in order to describe the system completely.

Let us see how this rule applies to our olivine system. Suppose we consider points in Fig. A-1 where only the liquid phase exists. The number of components is two (formally Mg_2SiO_4 and Fe_2SiO_4) and pressure and temperature are also variables. Hence with one phase and four variables (two components, temperature and pressure) we cannot specify the system unless we get, independently, three pieces of additional information. If we let pressure be atmospheric pressure (thereby establishing this variable) the system can be explicitly defined only if we further specify both the temperature and composition.

The extra required information is called the *number of degrees of freedom* and the general expression relating it to all the various quantities we have mentioned is called the *phase rule:*

$$\phi = C - P + 2$$

where ϕ is the number of degrees of freedom, C is the number of components, P is the number of phases, and 2 represents the two variables, temperature and pressure. Applying this rule to the olivine liquid (with no crystals) example given above we get: $C = 2$, $P = 1$, and $\phi = 2 - 1 + 1$ (pressure determined, hence no longer a variable) $= 2$. What is the number of degrees of freedom once olivine crystals form?

Another phase diagram of a simple binary system but *without* solid solution shows that crystals settling out of a liquid have a unique composition independent of the composition of the melt (Fig. A-2). If we cool a liquid enriched in component A relative to B as shown in Fig. A-2, the first crystals that will be formed are pure A. As the temperature falls, pure A continues to crystallize as the composition of the liquid changes in the direction B. At point e, crystals of both pure A and pure B begin crystallizing. The temperature is unique for the system at a specified pressure and is called the *eutectic* temperature. Crystallization will continue to completion at the eutectic at constant temperature, and the final amount of B relative to A will be proportional to the length of line ax relative to line bx, that is, the ratio in which the two were added to form the original liquid. If crystals were removed from the system during progress of crystallization, total composition and the proportions of A and B would also change.

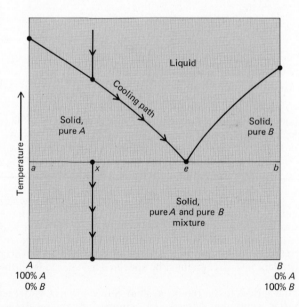

Figure A-2 Simple binary system phase diagram.

What we see in rocks are mainly the phases we call minerals (although glass, representative of the liquid phase, is also sometimes found). Rocks are rarely made up of one mineral or even as few as two minerals. They are commonly made of many minerals or phases. We can understand this fact when we consider the major components of a rock, which are generally listed as oxides since oxygen is the dominant element in the earth. Most rocks contain

SiO_2	Fe_2O_3 (and FeO)
Na_2O	CaO
K_2O	Al_2O_3
MgO	TiO_2
FeO	MnO_2

These ten components at constant temperature and pressure can be expressed in as many as ten phases before the system is rigidly defined. (Occasionally the presence of phosphorus, zirconium, or certain rare elements will result in additional phases.)

Appendix II
Constants and
Conversion Factors

PHYSICAL CONSTANTS

Speed of light in a vacuum	2.997925×10^{10} cm sec^{-1}
Avogadro constant	6.02252×10^{23} mol^{-1}
Electron volt (eV)	1.602×10^{-12} erg
Million electron volt (MeV)	1.602×10^{-6} erg
Atomic mass unit (AMU) = $^1/_{12}$ atomic mass of ^{12}C	1.6599×10^{-24} g
Mass of electron	0.0005486 AMU
Mass of neutron	1.0086654 AMU
Mass of ^{1}H	1.0078252 AMU
Energy equivalent of 1 AMU	1.492×10^{-3} erg
	931.5 MeV
Universal gravitational constant	6.670×10^{-8} dynes cm^2 g^{-2}
π	3.1416
e	2.7183

TERRESTRIAL CONSTANTS

Mass of the earth	5.976×10^{27} g
Area of the earth	510.100×10^6 km^2
Area of the oceans	362.033×10^6 km^2
Equatorial radius	6378.163 km
Polar radius	6356.177 km
Volume of earth	1.083×10^{12} km^3
Volume of oceans	1.350×10^9 km^3
Standard acceleration of free fall on earth	980.665 cm sec^{-2}

CONVERSION FACTORS

Meter (m) = 100 centimeters (cm) = 39.37 inches (in.) = 3.281 ft
Kilometer (km) = 0.6214 miles (mi)
Micron (μ) = 10^{-6} m = 10^{-4} cm
Centimeters per second (cm/sec) = 0.0360 km/hr = 0.0224 mi/hr
Liter (1) = 1000 cm^3 = 10^{-3} m^3 = 1.057 quarts
Kilogram (kg) = 10^3 grams (g) = 2.205 pounds (lb)
Microgram (μg) = 10^{-6} g
Year = 31,560,000 sec
2.303 log (base 10)x = 1n (base e or natural base)x
Calorie = 4.1840 joule = 4.1840 $\times$ 10^7 erg

Index